'In the aftermath of a global panden[...] brutality – both of which continue to [...] adverse impact on Black people – there [...] filled, need. We seek clarity and insight [...] minoritized Black people in leadership positions, in the 21st century. Michelle Moore's in-depth exploration represents a substantial contribution to the literature that addresses that need in an elegantly written, intelligent and accessible form. Michelle helps us to develop an understanding of how we can grow through our failures and recognise our successes. It's a manual to support us not just to survive, but also to thrive.'

Baroness Young of Hornsey OBE

'Michelle has written something that could simply change your life, views and old perceptions. Think, cogitate, discuss, reframe and reimagine; I dare you! *Real Wins* will deliver hard outcomes if implemented, but they do not dwell in the comfort zone. Be warned and be excited. Michelle explores mindsets, the effects of lessons learned, the power of sport and leadership and so much more. I picked it up and simply couldn't put it down as she weaves a rich tapestry from her own life and the insights and wisdom of those who have nourished her on the way. *Real Wins* will help us to unearth our ability to lead; it starts with ourselves and then the rest will be a new history.'

Colin Salmon, Actor

'This is a stirring, inspiring and precise guide to personal development, with many essential lessons on leadership and life itself.'

Musa Okwonga, writer

'Michelle Moore is an impactful force in conscious leadership and I am privileged to have been a beneficiary of her leadership influence, both in my life and in my career as a Black female professional athlete transitioning off the field into a new path of leadership in sport. *Real Wins* gives us insightful wisdom in how to navigate identity, inequality and success with the tools of self-awareness and resilience to run your own race.'

Eniola Aluko, Sporting Director, Angel City
Football Club and former professional footballer

'Michelle's formidable passion and thought-provoking style of leadership has helped redefine organisations in business and sport for several years. Her long-awaited book will not only inspire but challenge your way of thinking to bring out the best version of you.'

Denise Lewis OBE, Olympic heptathlon gold medallist

'Michelle writes a visceral and unapologetic book that lays bare truths that will help people to become the inclusive colleagues, leaders and community members that the world needs right now. Brace yourself and dive in.'

John Amaechi OBE, Organisational Psychologist and Founder of APS Intelligence

'In *Real Wins*, Michelle Moore provides a powerful and refreshingly honest account of what conscious leadership in the 21st century should look like. Blending personal anecdotes, interviews with leading figures from the world of sports, and critical thinking on effective and inclusive leadership, Moore has written a deeply humane and optimistic book. Moore demonstrates that when people inside organisations care enough to make sustainable change a priority, real change is possible. *Real Wins* is thus a must-read for those who want to become conscious leaders, both within sports and beyond. More than just a survey of leadership styles, *Real Wins* outlines practical strategies for success, including the necessity for self-care. As Moore argues, "effective leadership is grounded in authenticity, self-awareness and empathy for yourself and others". This brilliant and, at times, moving book provides a new model for leadership that will reshape the world of sports for years to come.'

Professor Ben Carrington, Annenberg
School for Communication and Journalism,
University of Southern California

'This is an important and exciting book that is truly of its time. Michelle captures the opportunity for an enhanced style of leadership and a better world for everyone where everybody wins. Who wouldn't want that?'

Kate Richardson-Walsh OBE,
Double Olympian and
former England Hockey Captain

'These dispatches draw on Michelle Moore's unmatched experience at the front line of social change, where sport meets education meets leadership. They provide an invaluable resource for anyone wishing to understand and to bridge the gap between easily-made statements of intent about fairness and the real, lived experiences of too many people.'

Chris Grant, former CEO, Sported and
independent board member, Sport England

'Michelle uses her sporting experiences, deep empathy, unique perspectives and solid leadership skills to inform and educate. It's exactly what we need right now. A no-nonsense approach to empowering us to lead with dignity, emotional intelligence and embracing our unique identities. Fabulous!'

Reshmin Chowdhury, journalist, broadcaster and event host, BT
Sport, Talksport and the BBC

'Michelle has been one of the most inspirational figures in education and sports leadership for over two decades now. *Real Wins* – exploring the intersection of race, sport and leadership – offers Michelle's wisdom, which has transformed the lives of young people, the careers of athletes and the culture of many organisations. A powerful and nurturing book and voice in the world of sport.'

Derek A. Bardowell, author of *No Win Race*

'*Real Wins* is a must read for anyone seeking an authentic leadership journey. Michelle uses her vast experience in sport and business to provide practical and insightful learning that will be invaluable in any leader's tool kit.'

Tunji Akintokun MBE,
business leader and philanthropist

'Written with passion, *Real Wins* is a personal and yet universal book filled with fascinating insights on identity, leadership and sport that will leave you challenged, uplifted and inspired to take action in new ways. It is a superb book by a remarkable woman, and is both courageous and timely. A must read.'

Ebony Rainford-Brent, World Cup
winning cricketer, broadcaster, Director of
Surrey County Cricket Club

'Michelle's indispensable wisdom and guidance will leave you inspired and empowered as she takes you on a journey of self-discovery to unravel, enhance and unleash your leadership potential. *Real Wins* is an important and compelling book packed with rich and universal lessons on motivation and success. Essential reading.'

Ama Agbeze MBE, International Netball player,
commonwealth gold medallist, former
England Netball Captain

'*Real Wins* is a riveting timely must read and call to action for anyone and everyone leading or wishing to lead in the global sport industry and beyond. Michelle Moore's raw, rich and reflective approach draws strength from her courageous honesty and vulnerability as she shares her experiences in and perspectives on the world of sport's battle with racial inequality and social justice. A book that challenges the reader to reflect on their own identity, sense of being and belonging.'

David Grevemberg CBE,
global sports leader and innovator

'Packed full of valuable leadership lessons, *Real Wins* is an inspirational and engaging read that left me exhilarated and motivated in new ways. Michelle shows us how to overcome challenges and find your way to be victorious.'

SSgt Clarence Callender OLY retired

Real Wins

*Race, Resilience and How to
Reach Your Full Potential*

MICHELLE MOORE

NICHOLAS BREALEY
PUBLISHING

London • Boston

First published in Great Britain by Nicholas Brealey Publishing in 2021
An imprint of John Murray Press
A division of Hodder & Stoughton Ltd,
An Hachette UK company

This paperback edition published in 2022

1

Chapter Six designs by Zem Clarke

A CIP catalogue record for this title is available from the British Library

Paperback ISBN 978 1 529 35964 0
eBook ISBN 978 1 529 35965 7
Hardback ISBN 978 1 529 35963 3

Typeset by KnowledgeWorks Global Ltd.

Printed and bound in Great Britain by Clays Ltd, Elcograf S.p.A.

John Murray Press policy is to use papers that are natural, renewable and recycla-
ble products and made from wood grown in sustainable forests. The logging and
manufacturing processes are expected to conform to the environmental regulations
of the country of origin.

John Murray Press   Nicholas Brealey Publishing
Carmelite House   Hachette Book Group
50 Victoria Embankment   Market Place, Center 53, State Street
London EC4Y 0DZ   Boston, MA 02109, USA

www.nicholasbrealey.com

Contents

For my grandparents, Olga and Vidal Moore and
Charlie and Margaret Mace, whose lives
have inspired mine.

In loving memory of Yvonne, gone too soon.

Foreword

I was nine years old when I first looked at the TV and felt seen. It was the 1992 Olympic Games in Barcelona. I was taken aback by the beautiful dark-skinned American women who ran like the wind, with a style and confidence that completely captivated me. Growing up as a young girl with sport as my guide, believing that I could be the best in whatever I turned my hand to, was so connected to that moment, because away from that space I didn't feel seen. Black women who looked like me were almost invisible.

When I first met Michelle, she had approached me to work alongside her with some young people in London, to empower them by sharing my story. The instant connection between us and her ability to not only understand the journey I've been on, but also have the vision to see how it could be used, is rare. Michelle is the confidant that I turn to help me walk in my purpose. A purpose which requires deep understanding of the nuance of being Black and a woman. So the honour of being asked by Michelle to write this foreword to a book this powerful is not lost on me.

The relationship between confident women of colour and leadership is complex, because it doesn't fit the status quo; it rides so hard against the grain that it makes things uncomfortable. The mental gymnastics of this begins at such a young age, as we navigate through overt racism, micro-aggressions and just generally having to learn things the hard way. It's an uncomfortable truth that we exist in daily. The coping mechanisms we exercise, just to blend into environments, and the code switching in order not to be hyper visible in situations, can be exhausting.

But how do we begin to own that space and be unapologetic? How do we take control of a narrative that can only be told by us? How do we lead from the front? How do we find our joy?

In *Real Wins* Michelle presents her answer to these questions with compelling clarity and precision. By positioning the voices of Black people, and Black women in particular, front and centre, *Real Wins* transforms the conversation. This is a compelling, universal and important book filled with deep insights, humour and inspiration.

I am a two-time Olympic finalist, five-time British champion, award-winning broadcaster and mother of two. Even as write that, I feel self-conscious of my own achievements, trying to silence my inner critic. I have listened to Michelle many times persuasively, in her own unique and motivating style, counter this narrative for me and so many others. In this book, Michelle does this by eloquently sharing her experiences, wisdom, and the stories of leaders and others who have been there before, to demonstrate how to overcome your own internal barriers and define success on your terms. *Real Wins* goes one step further and charts the ways to challenge the status quo whilst equipping leaders with the strategies to create spaces where everyone can be seen and succeed.

As an athlete I understood that my confidence was down to my ability as a sportswoman and being one of the best in the world. It has taken years to understand that my confidence is part of my overall identity. Sporting the red, white and blue of Team GB at an Olympic Games, I felt a level of respect from non-Black peers and those in other spaces who may otherwise have not looked at me twice.

As a broadcaster, life for me now means I shine a light on stories of people who have something to share; those moments are steeped in joy and pain, and can often be challenging. I have learned to lead in my field even if at times I didn't want to. *Real Wins* draws out some of these very complexities and at the same time shares strategies and potential solutions to find the courageous leader in all of us.

Michelle is unapologetic in the spaces she occupies, and I have seen first-hand the influence of her work and counsel. I remember a leading executive at major broadcaster discreetly asking me, 'What do you think Michelle thought?' after he nervously spoke at a media conference we both attended, he was so eager to impress. Needless to say, it would take a lot less talk and more action from him to impress Michelle. However, it made me smile inside and realize the power, authority and reach of her influence.

There is an urgency to Michelle's words in these pages. They pull you in, inspiring you to step up and be the change you want to see in the world. Using the fascinating experiences of athletes, activists, leaders and ordinary people Michelle has achieved something special in

Real Wins because this book will get you to think and then think again, providing you with the leadership fuel to win your own race on your terms.

Jeanette Kwakye MBE

Introduction

I was tired, really tired. That kind of bone-weary lethargy that is a legacy of exhaustion from those who have come before me. I'd just finished a 45-minute presentation to around seven hundred police officers, though it could have actually been a thousand. I was the last speaker on their diversity awareness day. In truth, I hadn't wanted to be there; in reality, it was the space where I needed to be. The previous day I'd struggled to make sense of the issues that I wanted to convey in a meaningful way that went beyond the same old diversity rhetoric, which I can't stand. I wanted it to be powerful. I'd called my brother Jean Pierre for advice; he told me to make it personal, make it about you and 'go all in'. That was the killer line that I'd needed to hear, but to be honest I was avoiding putting it into action. I was nervous because I knew that the presentation would take a lot out of me. As a Black woman, the emotional, intellectual and physical labour involved in revealing my personal testimony to move, challenge and inspire others can come at a cost to my wellbeing.

As I finished my last sentence on stage there was a moment of quiet, stunned silence before the polite applause. I've come to expect this now when expounding hard truths and calling out injustice: people are challenged, uncomfortable. My presentation was hard-hitting. It asked challenging questions of the police both as individuals and as an organization. I'd made it personal: Why did my ten-year-old nephew think it was normal for his dad to be stopped by the police? Why had so little changed in the police force in the decades since Stephen Lawrence's death in 1993? I'd shown them images of Serena Williams, Tommie Smith, John Carlos and Black athlete activists standing up in the pursuit of equality. I played them emotive and disturbing videos showing the harsh realities of living in 21st century Britain as a Black person: overrepresented in the criminal justice system, in mental health institutions and school exclusions. I knew I was leaving an impression; I could feel it – the tension, the anger at someone calling it out, some of the gasps. I felt the heat. A sea of white faces stared back at me from an audience that I could see included just one Black woman. Afterwards, she approached me, tears brimming in her eyes but not falling – such was her willpower. She expressed her heartfelt thanks, explaining that I'd said words that she couldn't say. This often happens in white spaces where there are lone Black folk; you become a party of two, if you're lucky. I always offer a listening ear in those snatched moments because we all want to be seen and understood, and never more so than by people who look like us. It took me weeks to recover from that presentation. I'd put everything I had into it, all of my experiences as a Black woman navigating the world.

John Carlos – the African American sprinter who at the 1968 Mexico Olympic Games who, alongside Tommie Smith, raised his fists in solidarity with the Olympic Project for human rights against the oppression of Black and Brown people worldwide – was once asked: 'How can athletes prompt change without jeopardizing their careers?' He replied: 'They can't. You have to lay it all on the line.'

***

Why did I write this book? The legacy of my ancestral oppression has given me a deep-rooted belief that my purpose is to challenge the status quo, and unapologetically so. To call out injustice. I've a lot to say but often feel censored – either by myself or externally.

At times there is a simmering anger to my words and in that an abject rejection of societal ills, and it's this combination that fuels my voice throughout this book. This creates a sense of urgency to my calls for action for each of us to take a stand and use our personal agency to unleash our best leadership qualities to contribute to making the world a better place. A healthy dose of realism, hope and inspiration are thrown into the *Real Wins* mix for good measure because that's my style as a sportswoman.

I talk about sport a lot. I use sport to explain life. I love sport. Not all sport but most sport. I play sport and, above all, am inspired by sport and the history of sport. Sport was the part of my childhood education that continues to give and give. Sport is escapism. It reflects you, and it reflects me. It has power, grace and wonder. Even the hardcore non-sport fan can't fail to be moved by the wildcard fairy-tale story of an unheard-of talent playing out their dream, defying the odds to beat the favourite to take the winning shot in the dramatic dying seconds. Sport crosses divides of time, place and peoples. Sport is my elixir; it both wipes the slate clean and holds an almost blinding light up to global injustices. Sport has gifted the world stand-out moments of protest, but I want more from sport, more specifically from the leaders of sport. Sport should and could be leading the way in fighting racial inequality – but it's not.

With age and experience, I've become more impatient for change, less forgiving, more strident and present to the harsh realities of racism and oppression that reduce the life chances of Black people, of women and of other people with marginalized identities. This injustice serves to fuel my journey as an activist, consultant, speaker and coach, working in sport and beyond to try to present solutions to age-old systems of oppression and bias.

There are many different faces to activism and its impact. I acknowledge that as a Black woman of mixed heritage my lighter skin affords me extra privilege compared to darker-skinned Black women when calling out bigotry and injustice. I intend to use my agency and influence for myself and this is my own offering of activism to the world. While societal ills can often make some of us feel like they are insurmountable, we all have personal agency and power that enables us to progress in life as individuals and thus, in turn, to build better societies that work for all of us. Learning how to utilize and harness that power and agency is what underpins much of this book.

At the heart of my work, I'm an educator. My first job 26 years ago was a primary school teacher and the elements that involved – of educating, supporting others and sharing – will never leave me. Through my leadership career in sport and education I have found myself giving advice. In the majority of my job roles, managers would ask me to support employees who were unhappy in their work environments. On top of this, I began collecting more and more mentees who seemed to benefit from my advice and words of encouragement. Today, based on my eclectic intersecting life experiences of leadership, sport and race, my leadership seminars and consultancy lay out the impact of oppression and life-limiting opportunities for those of us from Black and marginalized communities. Along the way I've been nationally recognized for my achievements, which has increased my visibility and therefore amplified the reach and power of some of my work.

In this book I want to challenge you to consider new ways of being and thinking when it comes to your own personal leadership growth and issues of race inequalities. In my professional capacity parts of my leadership coaching programmes are specifically for Black individuals while also providing strategic counsel to white conscious leaders to shine the light on the workplace inequities experienced by Black individuals as part of the workforce. This gives me a unique perspective while at the same time the experience of translating between the two. For my Black readers, some of the issues presented in this book will be well rehearsed, but they are framed within a self-leadership perspective which will serve to fortify and embolden you. For the white conscious reader, providing a lens for these issues and experiences will provide the nuance and potential solutions to uncover and unravel individual and collective responses to racism and oppression. This includes how to adopt effective inclusive leadership practice, although this book is categorically not a Diversity and Inclusion manifesto. This book is for anyone who cares about tackling racial injustice and is interested in leadership from both an individual and organizational perspective. I hear organizational leaders, especially those working in sport, say that when racism and discrimination are gone from society we won't have a problem in organizations. As banal as this sounds, it's worth highlighting: organizations are made up of people who make up society and people spend a lot of their time in organizations, so it stands to reason that we have to tackle the issue at an organizational level. By organizations, I mean corporations, sports, education, politics and community. I mean both the people and the leaders.

This book might be a wakeup call for some, but for everyone it's an opportunity to ask a different set of leadership questions. There is a vital need to have more nuanced and informed conversations about race. I use the word 'vital' because it is life and death. We need only remind ourselves of the alarming statistic that, in 21st century Britain, Black women are four times more likely to die from childbirth than white women. It's a statistic that never fails to take my breath away.

Throughout my professional career I've learned about compassionate, ethical and conscious leadership of oneself, teams and organizations, yet so much of my journey is rooted in the lessons I've learned from sport and experiences of exclusion.

My perspective is very simple. I am Black. I am also mixed. Some people would refer to me as 'mixed-race', but the term has never resonated with me. My dad was born in Guyana, South America. Guyana is classed as part of the Caribbean region because of its history under British colonial rule. My mum is from a leafy English town called Whyteleafe in Surrey. My mum met my dad in the 1970s. My paternal grandparents had travelled from Guyana in 1957 to make a new life in the UK. My nan who made this voyage was following her eldest daughter, my awe-inspiring Aunt Vilma, a nurse who had sailed to England as part of the Windrush generation. My nan travelled without her husband and with two young children, one my dad and the other my aunt. My family is filled with inspirational trailblazing women, and my nan Olga Moore paved the way. She survived the turmoil of a well-worn life to live to 93 years. My nan is my inspiration. I stand in her truths and on the shoulders of her history and rich heritage. I wrote and performed as a spoken-word piece at an event in 2018 to honour my nan's legacy: 'I feel the weight of injustice and oppression she endured. The harsh beauty of her courage, her resistance and, ultimately, her empowerment has been passed down to me.' It is this legacy that I believe emboldens my activism today, to call out injustice and speak the uncomfortable truths to those in powerful positions who knowingly or unknowingly uphold centuries of oppression and division.

My identity and sense of self were firmly cemented in some of these earliest childhood experiences of cultural traditions and love. As a young girl I saw myself – and still see myself – as Black. There is no confusion or equivocality about this, despite other people not always recognizing my Black identity because of my lighter-brown skin tone. Later on, the terms 'mixed-race' and, more latterly, 'Brown', which I have used at times (it's all about context), have become more commonplace. The politics of exclusion based on identity are heightened when they are so close to home that they form part of your own family dynamics. There were white members of my family who rejected my twin sister and me from an early age because of our paternal Guyanese heritage. This is very common in mixed-heritage families.

In the 1980s my dad's passionate urging that we boycott South African goods by not opening a Barclays bank account was cemented in my mind as an act we had to adhere to. Unknowingly as little Brown girls we were politicized. The writer and hip-hop artist Akala highlights in his book *Natives: Race & Class in the Ruins of Empire* how society racialized him as a Black mixed-race boy, just as it did my sister and me. Our dad was merely preparing us for that world while at the same time planting those early seeds of personal agency and protest, instilling the idea that our individual actions had meaning and impact. It's in that racialized world that from as young as four I remember my mum being abused in the street for having Brown babies – my twin and me. The campaigning work

I lead today is born out of a deep-rooted sense of racial injustice and a desire to honour the immense sacrifices and turmoil my mum endured. I slipped something in there – I hope you didn't miss it. I am a twin, and feel seriously extra special to have been included in the 1970s statistic of one in 250 births.

In the 1980s it was clear in my young mind that politically you were either White or Black. I was certain from my early experiences that I was not White, and that no 'Other' box on a census form would ever dupe me. When filling out a form to apply for a bank account, I remember being perplexed and angry over how ridiculous it was that it failed to provide a category for mixed people and in doing so demonstrated who belongs and who doesn't. Even at a young age I was not interested in submitting myself to government 'othering'. Under my dad's guidance and with my mum's support, a sense of individual agency was taking hold and becoming ever more firmly rooted as part of my identity. As a lighter-skinned Brown woman, I acknowledge that my experiences of racism and sexism are not as outwardly harmful as they would be for darker-skinned Black people. There are many different versions of Black, and I happen to be one. Contrary to what some people believe mixedness to be, my identity has never felt like a choice; it was and is a part of my experience of being in the world. I've never fitted in (sometimes quite literally, being six foot one) and have always been an outlier in all sorts of ways with my identity routinely and continually questioned. 'Where are you from?' South London is always my response, which is met with quizzical stares, 'No, I mean where are you *really* from?' Or, worse, 'What are you?' Those in the Black and mixed-heritage communities are only too used to – and exasperated by – this kind of questioning. People are really asking *how* Black are you? Where do your parents come from? In this way, they can figure out what box to put you in and how to treat you accordingly.

Growing up I desperately needed escapism from the said and unsaid questions of my identity. Enter sport! I was an athlete, a sprinter, a 400m runner. The athletics track has always been that place where I feel free, standing on the start line when all that matters is who is the fastest, who is the strongest, and who is going to win. From the age of ten my twin sister and I trained at Southwark Park athletics track in Bermondsey every Tuesday and a Thursday evening. I proudly wore the red and black stripes of the Herne Hill Harriers athletics club vest, competing at the weekends, revelling in the joy and freedom that running and winning gave me. We trained in the 'Blue', a part of Bermondsey known for its racism. My training group included young Black people with a smattering of white faces. I enjoyed the mixedness and sameness of identities. We escaped some of the racist abuse our Black friends were subjected to on those Bermondsey streets purely because we were lighter-skinned and always with our mum. I was a talented athlete. Described by my coaches as a 'trier' and, despite county success and a brief stint training in the United States, I failed to reach international standards. But athletics introduced me to the power of resilience against a backdrop of social, family and cultural challenge. I saw role models and people who looked like me 'winning', and I loved seeing them. When Tessa Sanderson became the first British Black woman to win Olympic gold, I celebrated in her success because my identity was wrapped up in her image.

We were well-behaved children, churchgoing, and quiet, studious types. We didn't have a lot of money: we lived in South London, on a council estate, a rough area but with a sense of community. It was a place which often felt tense, but it was home and people generally looked out for one another. There were too many dogs, and not just any old dogs – fearsome dogs; you know, the ones that quicken your step when you see them. Things would happen to remind us that we didn't live in an entirely safe place; it was an inner-city neighbourhood, after all. I was 15 and returning from training when I was shot by a pellet gun; it struck me in the back of my upper thigh. I screamed out in pain and shock when it happened, not that anyone heard or was around. It was a non-event, though not to me. I was shot for no reason, by someone hanging out of a window of a nearby block of flats. That's the kind of place we lived in.

Aged 11, there was a definitive moment where our vicar's failure to complete a school reference stating we attended the local church led to us missing out on a place at one of London's better girls' state schools, and instead we found ourselves at a Bermondsey comprehensive which struggled in academic performance. This was not a good start to my secondary education. Sometimes I wonder why the vicar failed to give us our reference – we went to church every Sunday, we were servers carrying the crosses and candles, but our service was not recognized by the vicar. We even worked some Saturdays at weddings, paid £1 for our time. It's only now in writing this book that my mum has told me that she thinks that the vicar may have had 'some issues' with Black people. He'd had a huge argument with my nan, and, given that we were one of only two Black families in the church, it all kind of makes sense. I'm not making any assumptions – actually, I think I am – but my point still stands that this is how racism works: it just hangs over something casting doubt and suspicion until it is proved. My nan was most probably standing her ground and using her voice as powerfully as she could.

At 12 we joined the Brownies, and this was problematic for two Brown girls. The Brownies are part of the Girlguiding organization for young girls. The Brownie leader barely concealed her distaste for us as the only Brown girls in the Brownie pack, often making racialized comments that I remember never quite understanding, even though I just knew she spoke to us and treated us differently from the other girls. She talked about us in odd ways. It was wasted on me, and I thought she was just weird. Being 'othered' is commonplace for Black children; these moments significantly affected me and are rooted in my psyche.

Those early personal experiences of the disparity that socio-economics and race played, and how they negatively impacted on my individual life chances and opportunities, lit an early unquenchable fire in me to champion my very own personal brand of unapologetic activism grounded in compassion and a desire to effect positive change in redressing inequalities.

Throughout *Real Wins* I do not try to speak for every Black person, but I do speak from a Black perspective, and there are times in this book when some things also apply to Brown and mixed folks. I also mention groups of people from other marginalized identities, based on gender, sexual orientation, disability, ethnicity, socio-economic background and religion. A word here on terminology. Language is ever dynamic and evolving and is personal, especially when talking about race; no language is perfect. I'm painfully mindful of this and at the same time frustrated by the incessant naysayers who pointedly refuse to evolve with the times as part of the 'political correctness gone overboard' campaign. There are many problems with colonized terminology – from the use of the word 'minority', when we've been minoritized by society, to the use of 'underrepresented' to describe groups of people, when we are underrepresented in the workforce only because we have been systematically excluded.

Real Wins has three central themes: race, sport and leadership. It might stand to reason that I would start my writing with some context setting around race as this provides the basis for some of my discussion points. However, Chapter 1, 'Redefining success on your terms', focuses on sport, mindset and leadership (and their intersections with race) because, for me, it's important that my writing – which is a reflection of my identity – is not only viewed through the lens of oppression. So, although it may seem slightly at odds with what's conventional, because this is *my* book and it's a part of who I am to do things differently, my book starts in this way.

Organizations bring me in to strengthen their people, to help unleash human potential and at the same time deliver a healthy dose of inspiration and motivation. I use the pain of my own struggles and the impact of oppression on me to offer solace, empathy and leadership career guidance to individuals whom I mentor and coach. Sport has provided me with a roadmap for success and an understanding of resilience in all of its forms. While affirming my identity, sport also delivered the life lessons that unleashed my leadership potential and the power to use my personal agency for good. Through my work in the world, I aim to create mini-ecosystems of warriors ready to take on the world, emboldened in new ways as transformers of their own lives and communities, often wielding a power they never knew they had.

I have written this book for the conscious leader in each and every one of us, supporting you while you examine different ways to enhance your own leadership potential, live into it, and flourish. I'm challenging you to think about, reflect on, discuss, reframe and reimagine some of your thinking on the issues presented.

The following chapters will unrefutably confront you with the truths about the realities of racial injustice and oppression. But they also contain hope and positivity. My message is grounded in optimism for individual and collective transformation, and will provide you with concrete, practical tips to make *your* difference in the world. That is why I have called the book *Real Wins*. As an athlete I value winning as key for so many reasons – the sense of achievement, motivation and fulfilment, the intrinsic satisfaction. Yet as a leader I have learned that a 'real win' isn't defined by the 'best of' or the winner; it's defined by the power of the lesson learned – by placing value on difference and evolution, on understanding the world from a different point of view from your own, and by holding the tensions of opposing views while still honouring yourself and others. It is only then that we can achieve personal and collective transformation. In figuring out the important lessons and having integrity we can recognize that we are all in need of dignity and empathy and that through our leadership journeys we get to choose how we respond to this in an ever-changing global community.

Real Wins is about grasping, grappling and overcoming fear and self-doubt to try something new. It's about conquering your own self-limiting beliefs to find new ways to define your own version of success and hold yourself accountable to that. When we set our own race, we can redefine our own boundaries for personal and professional success and be at peace with losing or failure. It's about those times we do lose and yet choose to be undefeated. Using stories from leaders who have risen through the ranks of sport and overcome multiple obstacles and from people who I have coached to success, alongside my own experiences, this book shares lessons on how to challenge stereotypes and tired assumptions to create your own winning formula. I'm invested in helping others achieve their personal bests in whatever form that might take. I want people to learn from my lessons, to be able to take their shot! Just like I was encouraged by my younger brother in my opening story to 'go all in', this is my invitation to you to find your own 'real wins' and ultimately to 'go all in'.

I talk to people all the time about taking up space, standing in their light, playing in the big leagues, WNBA-, NBA-style. My work is about standing in my truths, defining them, owning them and surrendering to the outcome. This book is my personal real win determined by my own definition of success: I invite you to take this journey with me.

Redefining success on your terms

'Will Michelle Moore, London team, please report to the officials hut immediately.' I heard the announcement and was worried. 'What have I done?' I was at the English Schools National Championships, representing London in the 400m. This was an important national track and field championship where all the regions compete to find the best athletes in the country. It was a big deal and felt like my very own Olympic Games. I had run my heat earlier in the day and had not made it through to the next round. I was a bit down ... well, more than a bit; I was disappointed in myself for not running faster. I trudged along to the officials hut at the back of the athletics stadium to be informed that I had run the same time as another athlete and would have to run a race off at the end of the day to see who would go through to the final for the next day. 'Are you sure you've not made some kind of mistake?' I asked the official in a disbelieving tone. He looked at me over his glasses and said, 'I know, luv. This has never happened before – you're making history.' He laughed and told me the time of the race. The news of the race-off went around the track meet like wildfire, with the other athletes excited by what they deemed to be a bit of drama. This was not helpful and raised my already heightened anxiety levels. I had 90 minutes before race time. I was excited and thankful for another chance. I was 16, and this was my first time away from home competing. It was all a bit scary but exhilarating at the same time. I felt truly alive. I was nervous, knowing the significance of being in an English Schools final could mean big things for my athletics career. Some athletes who make it to the finals can go on to achieve an international Great Britain vest. One of my rivals (now a friend), Donna Fraser, would be there, I was sure. The race-off had caused a stir among my London teammates, but I didn't want the fuss as I was anxious enough.

'On your marks,' the starter bellowed, my heart beating so fast I felt as though I had a microphone in my chest. Just before I got into my blocks, I clocked that my opponent was tall but not as tall as me. She was wearing red shorts. The sweat was starting to glisten on my upper lip, and I could feel it and wiped it away. I kept thinking that I didn't want to lose, especially in front of so many people who had stayed behind to watch. The gun went off and I got into my running, quickly letting my long stride gobble up the track. I reached the 200m mark with ease. There the London team was going crazy, shouting my name. 'Come on, Michelle!' they hollered. Their voices felt close, the wind carrying their voices around the top bend with me. 'Stay relaxed. Keep those arms pumping. You don't want to let coach down. You've got longer legs than her. Come on, you can do this, Michelle!' I kept repeating, 'Come on!', over and over again in my head, willing myself on.

As we approached the halfway point at 200m I could hear the patter of our feet beating the track down as our loping strides ate up the distance. We were level. My body felt at ease, my arms and legs effortlessly coordinating my actions. I started to coast around the top bend so I could conserve energy for the last 100m. Into the home straight we were neck and neck, but I could feel my legs becoming heavier and heavier. I was thinking, 'I haven't even started sprinting yet – what's going on?' The previous race and the two sets of warm-ups were taking their toll on my body. My legs felt heavy as if I was running through treacle. Latic acid had come for me, robbing me of my speed. I knew I was running out of time and felt as though I hadn't even started racing. All of this was going through my head as my stride length becoming shorter and shorter. I could feel my rival's looming presence next to me and then I felt it – a woosh of air on my cheek as she passed me in the last few metres of the race. I crossed the line and couldn't believe that I'd lost. It was over. I was devastated. I'd literally ran out of distance and time.

I was desolate but not surprised, as odd as that sounds. I was in shock that I could let myself down so badly. I was inconsolable and humiliated, the combination of the two almost too much to bear. There was nowhere to hide from such a public losing performance. I felt as though

I'd let everybody down: my coach, teammates and, above all, myself. I was in turmoil, busy berating myself with self-disdain and disgust for underperforming so dramatically, thereby rendering my training and sacrifice worthless. After my warm-down I traipsed back to the stands. Thankfully, most athletes had left. 'What happened?' my teammate Simone asked in the quiet and caring way she always did – which is why we were friends. I hung my head in shame and mumbled my 'I dunno' response. My embarrassment was as deep as the well I would've loved to have escaped into at that moment. The time for the race was one that I had run many times before, so I know it was well within my talents. I packed up my kitbag, which felt so much heavier than at the start of the day, plugged in my Walkman, and got on the coach, with my head down, my cap on so that everyone knew to leave me alone.

It's a loss I never truly recovered from, and I still feel it in my chest today some 30 years later. Looking back, I knew that I didn't have the winning mindset that day, or any other day I would soon come to realize. There had been the tell-tale signs such as being distracted by my opponent and falling into negative self-talk. I'd let the occasion get to me. I never forget that feeling of a wasted opportunity. I hadn't even given myself the chance to win because I didn't execute my race plan and had mentally checked out, rather than being in the present moment of the race. The race was a life-defining moment for me. I'd been under the spotlight and choked. I believe to this day that, if I'd given my best performance, the outcome might have been different; even if I didn't win, I would've known that I'd given my best efforts. That's the biggest regret I had: that I'd not seized the moment to realize all of my promising potential. The experience taught me about truly and deeply understanding the power of a winning mindset. The effects of that one race were long-lasting. My athletics career developed, and I became a decent county athlete, winning an inter-counties 400m race representing South-East England and training at the University of Southern California. But I never achieved the true international career success I dreamed of. My winning mindset was not strong enough, and I'd let the fear of failure determine my future success in all kinds of ways. I gave up athletics eight years later when I decided to focus on my teaching career.

As a speaker I must have told this story a hundred times, and each time I tell it people expect the ending to be victorious. Stories of success over failure are fundamentally what people want to hear. But it is failure that teaches us the most about self-belief and how to compete for your own personal best. The lessons we gain from failure paradoxically become your 'real wins'.

I've won some races and lost some. Sport has been and continues to be a great teacher. From a young age it taught me that to win I needed to leave everything on the track in all of my best efforts while at the same time accepting that I might lose in the process. It was a lesson learned too late for my English Schools race-off, but that lesson is something we can all apply to our lives, though it requires a particular mindset.

Understanding the mindset of an athlete can help you to manage and cope with failure in your everyday lives, and, in turn, helps you to define success on your own terms. The operative words here are 'own terms' because success and winning look and feel differently for each of us. By understanding what it means to fail you are able to keep moving forward. That's why failure is so important and integral to winning at work, on the sports field and in life.

The mindset of success

Conquering a mindset for success for that winning performance in life can be achieved by anchoring positive thoughts and mantras. The concept here is known as illeism, which is the act of talking to or about yourself in the third person. This self-talk strategy helps athletes to distance themselves psychologically from the situation and increases their ability to regulate their emotions. Illeism is often practised by sportspeople, including Anthony Joshua, Raven Saunders, Andre Agassi and Pelé. Research has shown it is a beneficial technique to improve performance. You can use this strategy especially where you lack confidence in certain situations. For example, through applying illeism you can coach yourself to resolve a conflict with a colleague and take it one step further by stepping into a different persona altogether. You can create an alter ego; you can name him/her and step into that assertive and more reassured persona in those moments when you want to feel and appear more confident. This strategy works well with people who are more introverted in their nature and find it tricky to assert their views, especially at important times.

My friend and previous rival on the track, Olympian Donna Fraser, has used illeism in her sporting career and life with powerful effects. Donna has an alter ego called Diane, and when I interviewed Donna, I expected her to tell me about how Diane helped her win on the track, but it went deeper than that. Donna is a breast cancer survivor, and it was the power of positive self-talk in the third person through Diane that helped Donna adopt a positive mindset. In Donna's words: 'When I was told about my diagnosis, I cried a bit, but then Diane quickly took over and told me to fix up, look sharp, and from that moment on I applied myself to doing everything I could to help myself live.' Donna is a huge inspiration to me and many. After a successful career in sport, she now leads the equality and diversity work for UK Athletics. Donna achieved the Freedom of the Borough honour for Croydon in 2019 and an OBE for services to equality in the workplace in 2020.

Illeism isn't the only psychological trick we learn from sporting greatness. According to the eminent psychology professor Carol Dweck, adopting a growth mindset for success in life is one of the determinant factors in creating a positive inner belief system. A growth mindset describes people who believe that their abilities can be developed through effort and are open to learning and tackling problems. The best sportspeople and most successful people in professional life have a growth mindset. By contrast, those people who have a fixed mindset believe that abilities are fixed, leading them to avoid challenges and to lack confidence to adapt to new circumstances. My race-off defeat was a result of the pressure I had put on myself: rather than allowing myself to rely on the fact that I could complete the race in a time that I'd achieved in the past, my perception of the task had magnified the intensity and stress of the moment. In sports psychology this is about separating motivation from pressure. Let me explain.

There is another important aspect to growth mindset: the need to focus on the process rather than the outcome of your motivation or desires. This applies to the sports arena as much as it does to any significant, testing moment. In a race scenario this is about concentrating on the elements of the execution of the race rather than on your position at the end of the race. Focusing on the victory can add to the pressure the athlete feels whereas sticking to the game plan allows him or her to control the fear associated from the perceived pressures. A high-profile athlete may feel pressure from the media, spectators and others expecting them to do well. If an athlete interprets these elements as a threat to their potential victory, this results in heightened anxiety, which can have a debilitating effect on performance. Taking control of this requires the athlete to change their perception of pressure and to view it as a challenge to overcome. They can then begin to understand that what is being asked of them is their profession: something they have worked hard for and is second nature and therefore achievable.

My interview with the Olympic sprinter and now sports broadcaster Jeanette Kwakye illustrates how a growth mindset and how aspects of illeism operate in real time. Before her World Indoor championship 60m final in 2008 in Valencia her coach asked her to write the headline for the newspapers for the next day. Jeanette wrote: 'Kwakye breaks British record.' He then asked her to focus on the race game plan, and that was it. The plan worked, and Jeanette went on to claim silver medal in the final, breaking the British record and becoming British champion, placing Jeanette at number two in the world at that time. Jeanette was able to conquer her fears by externalizing them through the act of writing that newspaper headline, enabling her to stop internalizing the fear which was negatively impacting her mindset. This released her focus on negative feelings, empowering her to break free from their hold on her. Literally giving away your fears to your 'third person', or spilling your fears into a diary or an imaginary newspaper headline so they are no longer a part of you, is a powerful mindset shift that can create extraordinary results in your life.

The Great Britain track and field heptathlete Katarina Johnson-Thompson thought about quitting the sport when she failed to win a medal at Rio 2016 Olympic Games. The British media had documented her ongoing setbacks with injury and poor performances since 2014. It was agonizing viewing as millions tuned in to see her foul out in the long jump in the Beijing 2015 World Championships, and then, in the Rio 2016 Olympic Games, disaster had struck again with a breakdown in the javelin. At the London 2017 World Championships, the newspaper pages carried pictures of Katarina with her head in her hands in the high jump bed, having failed three attempts at what would usually be an easy height for her to clear, thereby dashing all hopes of medal glory.

Katarina was clearly and still is a talented athlete, at that time set to follow in the footsteps of heptathlete royalty Jessica Ennis-Hill and Denise Lewis, but she couldn't quite overcome her anxieties and poor performances. She had to take a leap of faith and made big changes by changing coaches and relocating to France. It paid off, and at the Doha 2019 World Championships she won gold and broke the British record with a score of 6,981 points, which ranked her at number 6 on the all-time heptathlon lists. After her gold medal performance, *The Guardian* ran the headline, 'I've cried enough to last me a lifetime', under which Katarina reflected on her long road of adversity to the gold medal. Her words resonated deeply with me and reminded me of the young and sometimes emotional athlete I once was. For Katarina her journey to gold was littered with many failures. She displayed real courage in the face of such public failure and was prepared to make big changes and sacrifices in turning her life around and finding a new path to her ultimate gold medal glory. She displayed all the characteristics of a growth mindset – something that's available to all of us. When you have a growth mindset you are open to learning new ways of thinking and taking on board feedback to improve performance, whether that's on the sports field or in the workplace.

The beautiful thing about failure is that it provides the perfect gift of feedback. As an athlete, each time I competed my coach would tell me exactly what I'd done wrong, so from a very early age I was accustomed to receiving constructive feedback as part of the training to win. Races are won by one thousandth of a second, unless, of course, you're Usain Bolt and you give your opponents a glorious smile as you pass them in the dying metres of the race. Marginal gains are the micro adjustments you make to your technique and mindset in order to achieve your peak performance in preparation for victory. When I'm working with people helping them to prepare for important job interviews or presentations, I introduce the concept of marginal gains. This can take many different forms. It could be putting yourself into a peak mindset by doing an activity just before you start that gets you into a state of high vibration. This can include everything from listening to music to meditating, and is different for everyone. The biggest marginal gain to be found, however, is in your mindset shift of facing up to your fears. There's more on this later.

Tools of resistance

The beautiful thing about failure is that it provides the perfect gift of feedback.

Using a sporting mindset can provide many life lessons for managing failure or adversity in your professional working life. To highlight this, in the table below I've broken down the elements of my negative mindset traps which contributed to my race-off loss. These traps can be applied to the professional settings you can find yourself in. Included, too, are the countering positive mindset techniques.

Disruptors/negative mindset	Positive mindset
I had lost sight of my race plan and failed to execute it.	Do you forget your innate skills, talents and competencies to achieve your professional and personal life goals? Give yourself a reality check by displaying a list of what your core strengths are somewhere you can see it every day. *MM Inspiration:* 'You are talented, have a plan and can do this.'*
I had let voices of self-doubt creep into my mindset and the pressure get to me: I was distracted by environmental factors including the physique of my opponent, the behaviour of my teammates and my internal negative self-talk.	How often do you focus on all the elements that add to the pressure you feel and on the things that could go wrong rather than what could go right? It's widely recognized that what you focus on expands, so if you think more about failure than success, then you're more likely to fail than to succeed. This drains mental energy towards thoughts that don't elevate you. Try practising illeism. *MM Inspiration:* 'You got this.'

Disruptors/negative mindset	Positive mindset
I had mentally checked out and performed in autopilot mode.	Do you experience moments when you're in the room but not really in the room because you've let fear dominate you? Reimagining possibilities and visualizing yourself excelling and expecting your own success is the key to unlocking your potential. Practise visualization techniques by seeing yourself winning in your mind's eye. Feel the emotions of the victory. *MM Inspiration:* 'If you see it and feel it, you can believe it and achieve it.'
I'd let the fear of failure determine my future success.	How often do you let failure define you and therefore make fear-based decisions that negatively impact your future? Consider adopting a growth mindset, in the knowledge that fear is often an illusion and can be reframed by considering the potential positive outcomes as opposed to the 'What if' negative scenarios that may never happen. Afford yourself the gift of reimagining possibilities. *MM Inspiration:* 'Keep it real.'

* My motivational coaching streak always comes out with my words of 'MM Inspiration'.

Tools of resistance

The odds may appear to be stacked against you, but it is in this struggle and through the lessons learned that the power of a winning mindset emerges, creating a burning desire to overcome and excel.

Identity and failure

As a young woman, athletics was the first place I felt comfortable in my own skin, where I was surrounded by fellow Black athletes. Athletics affirmed my identity, and it was my happy place, so when I lost a race, it was an exacerbating experience because it was in such contrast to the joy the sport gave me. My disappointment didn't last for long, though, as there was always another competition in the fixtures calendar to train for. I moved from one loss to a potential win at the next competition: a 'real win' life lesson of dusting yourself off and focusing on the very next opportunity. In my case, it was the next race; in yours, it might be the next business pitch, job interview or sensitive conversation with the teenager in your life. Whatever it is, the key to managing failure is rooted in how we choose to move forward. That's the life skill that sport gifted me.

Then there are those tough moments in sport when athletes have to make the winning shot, putt, penalty shootout, or basketball or netball shot in the dying seconds of the games, and they miss. They could easily be consumed by that miss the next time they are in the same position, but the best athletes use it as their fuel and don't let it impact their future performance; they develop the resilience to not only shrug it off but to process it which then allows them to move on to try again, fail again and eventually succeed.

Many of us have chalked up losses in our professional lives. Failure is a bitter pill to swallow whole. This is more complicated when it comes to the issue of race. This is because of the barriers and oppressions faced by Black people in the workplace, while being held accountable to a higher and different set of standards compared to their white counterparts. Black people are given less chances to succeed. We only need to look at the record of Black football managers in English football. As soon as a team run by a Black football manager starts to lose, they are sacked and struggle to find a new position. Their white counterparts, by contrast, are given many more chances if they fail, and get to move on time and time again and walk into future management positions. There has been a total of just nine Black managers in the history of the Premier League. Likewise, researchers at Arizona State University's Global Sport Education and Research Lab have identified that coaches of colour have more significant and relevant playing experience than their white counterparts and yet do not receive equivalent 'second chances' When African American head coaches have been fired in the National Football League (NFL), it has been more difficult for them to obtain another head coaching position at the same level.

Dealing with losing is part of the beautiful game, and is never felt more strongly when you layer this with the intersectional burden of race and gender that Hope Powell had to contend with as England's first Black female football manager. After a successful playing career involving 66 England appearances, Hope became not only the first female football manager in 1998 but England's first Black manager in the men's and women's game and the first woman to earn a UEFA Pro Licence. Back then, Hope had to not only be the head coach and manager but also create an entire girls' and women's structure for England. Hope is a pioneer of the women's game, yet the sport is so steeped with racism and sexism that she remains England's sole Black female football manager, now working at Brighton & Hove Albion women's team in the Women's Super League.

For Black football managers and for any marginalized community to overcome failure, we have to be more creative, enduring many false starts and being forced to find new arenas of possibility – all this while negotiating their way through the emotional juggling necessitated by multiple injustices. It's the classic account of people from marginalized communities who become the outliers in their fields – the First of Difference, a term coined by super producer Shonda Rhimes in her book *Year of 'YES'*. Oppressed people understand that these additional barriers have to be taken into account when viewing success and failure because society is telling them that they have to be better than the dominant culture. For oppressed groups, this becomes a part of the mindset approach to dealing with resistance and failure.

For this book I had the honour of interviewing Lola Young, Baroness Young of Hornsey, who talked about her experiences overcoming barriers and the turmoil of a background of adversity growing up in the care system from the age of eight weeks to 18 years old. I was so moved by her words, and as one of a very small number of Black women in the House of Lords her contribution to British society has been, and is still, immense. What struck me when Lola talked was her utter refusal to accept how society, patriarchy and racism positioned her and how she learned to reconstruct her own positioning in the world. In entering rooms of power and privilege knowing that she was going to be the only Black person, Lola would always ensure that she was overprepared, reading and rereading papers, preparing cross-examination questions and being able to expertly cut through and succinctly summarize complex issues. When I reflected on Lola's words, I realized what she was saying was more complex than just having to be overprepared (which is something I relate to). Her labour is demonstrative of the outsider status any oppressed group can feel where you are constantly checking your positioning for the environment you find yourself in. The lesson I took from her wise words is that, despite the constructs those of us from marginalized identities may find ourselves forced into, finding the inner courage and resilience to not be defined by their limitations is what creates the mindset for success and wellbeing. Being on the margins informs, but does not determine, the stance we take.

Professor Emeritus Kevin Hylton is part of the fewer than 1 per cent of UK professors who are Black. When we spoke, Kevin explained to me some of the ways in which he disrupts racism. He, too, adopts a mindset based on excellence. When he is not in his academic robes, he finds that his credentials are sometimes questioned. He may not meet the norm for leaders in senior positions. Therefore, he makes sure that he subtly weaves in his background and experience as a leading academic and author, in order to demonstrate – to those who don't know him and who may perhaps be unfairly judging him – that he is often overqualified to be in the room. I couldn't believe I was hearing this from a man of such distinction.

There is an age-old conversation many Black families have with their children: 'You have to be ten times better than your white counterparts.' I have to admit I do find the sentiment of excellence problematic and exhausting, but I accept that this is our lived reality today. At a deeper level I want to reject it because of how unjust and labour intensive it is. It exhausts me to think that I have to be ten times better than my white counterparts; it makes me want to stop writing. It's evident that I didn't, though, because, after all, you're reading this. The façade of meritocracy can at times make it tough to step up. Hearing and seeing stories of Black success overcoming hardship and challenge serves to inspire many – to help them defy and exceed expectations despite the barriers and blockades of oppression. Such is the cultural power and capital of Black heroes and sheroes they can become instrumental in reimagining your own success through their success and in turn become inspirational agents of survival and hope to Black communities.

Losing or failing at something can serve to add more ammunition to our efforts and boost our mindset so that we achieve against the odds. Seeing high-profile Black athletes or public figures lose or fail either out on the court or pitch or in business is hard-hitting to witness because, as a fellow Black person, you're invested in their success: you see yourself in them and recognize your and their shared cultural history, knowing the intersecting barriers of oppression they would have faced to get to that point. So, when they lose, the loss takes on a deeper significance.

Tools for leaders

Organizational leaders must be cognizant of our different starting points while also having a deep understanding of the lie that is meritocracy.

That's why working-class hero Ian Wright was, and still is, a popular figure as one of England's best Black footballers. When you witnessed the magic of his famous goals, often on the end of compatriot Mark Bright's cross, the Black community celebrated in him and for him. When a Black athlete is victorious, the exultant achievement takes on greater significance for the Black community, the joy of the win becoming representative of the Black collective struggle and liberation, as described by acclaimed Professor Ben Carrington, 'Sport engages the ludic, the play element within, in order to show us what it means to be free – a freedom that exists, however temporarily'. It shows us, as suggested by Professor Ben Carrington, what it means to be free. The sports arena becomes a space which offers Black people freedoms that are rarely felt or offered in wider society.

Tools of resistance
For Black people using the context of pain and points of
our difference to succeed against the odds is part of our
histories and the legacy of struggle.

Facing the fear

I like to think of mistakes as an evidence trail of personal
resilience: there are the times you've beaten the odds and
the times you haven't. Failure can teach you to look through
your past experiences, and by finding ways to confront it
you can find ways to defeat it. Your failures and even to
some extent your pain become valuable life resources. In
checking and rechecking your experiences of failure, you
provide yourself with a dossier that you've been there
before, that you've overcome something once, and you
can do it again and that you have acquired enough self-
efficacy – belief in your ability – to achieve your goals in
any situation. The psychologist Albert Bandura described
these beliefs as determinants of how people think, behave
and feel. When I received the news that the publisher loved
my proposal and wanted to publish this book, as a new
author I felt daunted at first. However, I comforted myself
with the knowledge that I'd written a great deal before,
including articles, educational curricula and three disserta-
tions. By presenting myself with my life's evidence trail, I
developed the confidence to help me write this book. All
of this could be described as my having high self-efficacy
levels, although it didn't rid me altogether of my nervous-
ness about embarking on the writing voyage!

Failure teaches you about your own fears and vulner-abilities. The writer and acclaimed research professor Brené Brown asserts that you have to allow yourself to experience the pain that goes with failure and not to find spaces to avoid it. Brown calls this 'braving the wilder-nesses'. This kind of vulnerability is something we could all learn from because there is truth and strength in open-ing yourself to your fragilities and understanding them. Understanding this enables you to look through your past experiences of failure. Feeling fearful is common to so many of us especially at those important life moments, and for some of us it's a daily occurrence. We can spend inordinate amounts of time analysing our fears; I know I have. However, our fears are communicating to us that we have a deep desire and want for something and can be a sign that we're on the right path.

When you give into your fears, you can lapse into staying in your comfort zones and never truly living the life that you want. There is nothing wrong with comfort zones, but we just can't be in one all the time. When I worked in one of my public sector roles, I would meet people who were genuinely happy in their jobs and I remember feeling envious that it wasn't the same for me; I was just not happy enough. 'Enough' being the main word here. Sport had taught me to get the most out of my body and my mind, so my internal wiring wanted this for my professional career, too. I always wanted more, even if I didn't really always know what 'more' was. All I knew was that I wasn't fulfilling my potential.

Having been in the same organization for a number of years, deep down I was scared of the unknown and change. You may be able to relate to this and may have asked yourself similar internal phrases and questions to the ones that ran daily through my brain: 'This can't be it ... There's got to be more.' On the face of it I should have been content – I was well paid, in a leadership role, had autonomy and my work was making a difference for communities – but I was still discontent. Eventually, life just became too uncomfortable, so I sought new opportunities and secured a new role and developed my consultancy. A number of years down the line I wonder why I left it so long. I believe it was because I had been operating in my comfort zone for a long time and needed the pressure of being stretched. Perhaps you've spent too long in your comfort zone, staying in an unrewarding job or getting stuck in an aspect of your personal life.

Tools for leaders

Everyone needs to be operating in their stretch zones at some point because peak performance occurs when you stretch. You cannot grow unless you stretch.

Success strategies

When you make those changes and reach your goals, the work doesn't stop. Organisational psychologist and former NBA basketball player John Amaechi OBE uses a fitness metaphor to describe this: success is the getting into shape part, but once you've reached your goal, you have to maintain your fitness efforts. In the same way, when defining and reaching your professional and personal goals of success, you should avoid falling into the trap of thinking that the work stops there, especially when it comes to high achievement. This doesn't mean you can't be highly competitive and strive for that gold medal, job promotion or highly desirable car. It just means that you take on board the fact that, once you've achieved your goal, there has to be an ongoing process of learning, working and balancing on a constant repeat cycle if you are to continue to achieve and be successful on your own terms. The way the brain works is that, once you've achieved that goal, you immediately move on to the next one, rather than celebrating and acknowledging that achievement for its magnitude in that moment and as part of the continual journey of success and education. You often move on to all the drama of achieving the next big thing. It's our reptilian brain at work. As the saying goes, 'Remember when we said we wanted what we have now?'

Tools for leaders

Success is a continual mode of operation with regular pitstops and occasional moments of achievement. It's an ongoing process of learning, growing, ravelling and unravelling, and working to reveal your best efforts and sometimes uncover hidden talents.

All of us have times of self-doubt, anxiety, overwhelm or fear, but how do we ensure that we don't spend too long at these 'train stops' and potentially become derailed? Acceptance is, I believe, the answer. There's power in accepting and understanding that, in life as in work, you will experience resistance, setbacks and failures and you will make mistakes. *Nobody* is exempt from these experiences. It's not about expecting that something will go wrong; it's developing the mindset that deeply understands that resistance is part of the process, and that it will always make a guest appearance, sometimes in a major part, at others in a minor role. Often, it's essential to the overall plotline, providing you with the secrets (for your eyes only) that will strengthen your final performance. The fear that often comes with the resistance is sent to motivate you to go forward or change direction, and coupled with acceptance it liberates you to get on with life regardless of the barriers you face.

Understanding that resistance is often an essential part of the process that will strengthen your final performance can be key. The New Thought minister and writer Michael Bernard Beckwith asserts that, when you feel as if circumstances and situations are pressing in on you, the only way to overcome them is to go within and ask yourself a set of empowering questions: 'What is my purpose?', 'What is my gift to share?' and, my own adaptation, 'What is the lesson here?' These are distinctly different questions from 'Why me?' or even 'What should I do?' Michael emphasizes that asking empowering and sincere questions of yourself or to the universe results in answers that are sent to you in a language you'll understand – in signs, intuitive hints, inner promptings or dreams. I like this exercise because it is available to each and every one of us in whatever situation we find ourselves in, especially if we are trapped in our own minds by an event that happened in our past such as a failure or mistake. Whether you believe in the awareness of a universal presence or not, the notion of asking yourself the bigger questions provides a new way of viewing your problem to give you space and time to reflect more deeply on the potential solutions.

This was demonstrated in my interview with England's first Black female cricketer, Ebony Rainford-Brent, when she shared with me how she learned about empowering self-questioning as a way to take control of a life-debilitating back injury that stopped her playing cricket for three years.

At 19, Ebony suffered a prolapsed disc in her back and she lost the ability to walk. The following three years of rehabilitation were marked by bouts of depression but also self-actualization. Ebony describes these years as providing one of her most valuable life lessons, as she moved from asking herself over and over again why this had happened to her to posing the more liberating, future-facing question 'What small steps can I take right now to get better?' Rainford-Brent told me that it was then that she learned about the power of the mind and how asking yourself the right questions at times of crisis can shape your experiences. Ebony went on to become a World Cup winner, an acclaimed presenter and award-winning campaigner.

In her interview with me, Eniola Aluko – a former professional footballer, at one time one of the best strikers in the world, and now sporting director for US Angel City football club – revealed something similar. As a sportswoman, she says, she built a winning mindset through the power of visualization, by picturing herself scoring and putting the goal in the back of the net. This is, of course, a well-known technique in sport, but something more interesting emerged when she added: 'Most people don't allow themselves to feel that place of fear.' The place of fear is the potential failure, but once you've faced that fear down you can deal with whatever outcome comes your way. In doing this you actually liberate yourself to visualize and imagine your win and realize that victory can be achieved.

Tools of resistance

When you free yourself from the fear of failure and accept it, you become more aligned with your life and the signs it gives you, more resilient and readier to deal with resistance when it shows up even when you don't want to.

The power of focus

'I think it's helpful to focus on what we can control, so let's look at what those things are for you.' I was talking to Zion, the secondary school teacher I was coaching through the microphone attached to my laptop. I was trying to convey encouragement and positivity. Zion met my eyes with a blank stare, and I could hear the words he wasn't saying through his sardonic facial expressions: 'Tell me something I don't know, will you?' It was mid-April 2020, and in the UK we were in the midst of a COVID-19 lockdown. In response to the global pandemic, children were at home and teachers were teaching the curriculum online. A large number of my planned contracts of work had been cancelled, so I had had to adapt my consultancy services by creating a new coaching and mentoring programme to strengthen the personal and professional resilience of teachers and the school workforce. As individuals, we couldn't control the decisions the UK government were making, the course of the virus or the economic devastation left in its wake, but we could control our response to it and how we chose to focus on our skills, abilities and strengths to look after ourselves and those around us.

It's fair to say that Zion was a bit resistant to my ideas. As I broke some of his resistance down, however, Zion's body language started to change: he sat up straighter and became more engaged. We focused on the resources he could use to teach more effectively and how adopting some positive mindset techniques and prioritizing his wellbeing would help him to show up more authentically for the children. It stands to reason that you need to ensure your emotional health and wellbeing needs are catered for before you can be fully present to the needs of others.

I'd based my coaching on some of the teachings of the educator and writer Stephen Covey. I was first introduced to the book *The Seven Habits of Highly Effective People* in 2004 on a FranklinCovey leadership course. The main premise of Stephen's book is based on how proactive people focus their energy and time on the things they can positively do something about. Stephen describes this through two concentric circles: the Circle of Concern and the Circle of Influence. The larger, outer Circle of Concern represents everything you care about – that is, your family, health, career, finances, world events. The smaller, inner Circle of Influence represents all the concerns you can actually proactively do something about. He says proactive and effective people focus on the Circle of Influence, where they work on the things they can control, which ultimately enhances their wellbeing

Zion was angry and upset about the high numbers of schoolchildren at home who had no access to a computer. His school was in an inner-city area and was suffering from government cuts so there was no funding to purchase new computers. By focusing on some of his key strengths of organization and advocacy, Zion was able to successfully crowdfund and raise £10,000 (almost $14,000) to purchase new computers for his students. All of this came out of a coaching conversation about what's possible when we focus on what we can control rather than what we can't.

Non-attachment

Early on in my career I was often called a control freak and a worrier; Stephen Covey's work has helped me to manage this, but what has had an even bigger impact on my life is releasing my attachment to the outcome of some of my deepest desires. Yes, this does sound counterintuitive, but the practice of non-attachment is a philosophical tradition of long standing. Many of us have been in positions where we desperately want a positive outcome from the career promotion, the funding agreement or the question 'Will you go out on date with me?' When we are fiercely attached to the outcome of something we don't currently have, it creates a heightened eagerness about and expectation of that thing. However, even if we do achieve the 'Yes' we so urgently want, we have built it up to such a degree that it loses its attraction, and we are left feeling curiously bereft and disenchanted. Practising the principle of non-attachment is about releasing your attachment to the outcome of your desires. This doesn't detract from your investment and burning aspirations; it just means you offer up your personal best and let the chips fall where they may. This creates a process which is more grounded in the here and now of the moment rather than focused on the outcome. It's a more liberating and reassuring experience of striving for success. If only I'd known this on the day of my England Schools race-off!

Three years ago, my brother Jean Pierre landed an interview for his dream job working for the London Mayor as part of the youth crime prevention team. I helped him through his application process. To say that Jean Pierre wanted the job was an understatement; I'd never seen him more motivated. The work encapsulated all of his passions for young people and crime prevention, linking social policy and community development. Jean Pierre knew his stuff, and was experienced enough and well suited for the role. However, because it was a highly sought-after role with a number of interview stages, Jean Pierre needed to find a way to deal with his nerves and feelings of self-doubt that were clouding his thinking. So, instead of worrying about the end goal, I encouraged him to focus on all the elements he *could* control, namely his mindset. I supported Jean Pierre in his preparation, helping him to realize that, while he couldn't control the end outcome (he couldn't force the panel to want him or even like him), he could control his behaviour and thought process during the interview itself. In focusing on communicating his passions and ideas instead of trying to persuade the panel to choose him, he was able to master his mindset. Jean Pierre took control of the interview situation by accepting and surrendering to whatever the outcome, confident in his own value, abilities and energized by the joy of sharing his passions. In the letting go of the outcome he released himself of fear and self-doubt. The interview panel saw and felt that energy and confidence and offered him the job.

Success is made up of a thousand failures and setbacks. Building an acceptance that these are in fact valuable lessons will ultimately create a tapestry of rich life experiences and personal-best winning moments.

Real wins

- Success and failure are of equal importance, and your reaction to both is what ultimately leads you to reward and fulfilment.

- Externalizing and facing your fear of failure is the key to a winning mindset.

- Understanding the context of your full identity and points of difference can be one your biggest strengths in succeeding.

- The mindset for peak performance is accessible to all of us.

2

Can you see me?
(In)visibility

I felt as though I was being suffocated and I couldn't fight back. It felt frighteningly real. Thankfully it wasn't. A mighty force was pinning me down, and I could feel this irresistible weight much like a sledgehammer slamming me relentlessly into the bed mattress. My muscle strength was non-existent and no match for this kind of opponent. I focused on fighting the urge to struggle, as I knew that this was the way I would release myself from the moment ...

I was having a night terror – one of those disturbing dream-state experiences where your conscious mind is active but you're actually still asleep. I've had a number of them throughout my life, all at points of extreme stress. In this instance I had been passed over for a promotion at my workplace. In reality, I was demoted without even realizing it until it was too late. I'd taken my eye off the ball of my own career path, and instead I'd been focusing on those of my team, managing their roles at the expense of my own.

I was looking out for everybody else, but nobody was looking out for me. As a former athlete, the pursuit of winning is in my bones and etched into my DNA. This demotion felt like a loss on epic proportions, akin to taking over the relay baton on the fourth leg anchor in first place position and then dropping the baton and getting the whole team disqualified. On this occasion I was too tired to be 'warrior woman'; perhaps I had chosen defeat over winning. It was a big wakeup call. From that point on, I began to focus on what I could control – my own work. I let it speak for itself, and within the year my work had received national acclaim. As a consequence, new opportunities arose, and I was able to make my own demands to redress the previous inequities. This was a real win on my terms.

The experience taught me about how Black and white women are seen, heard and understood. Race had played its part in my demotion; my white women counterparts were rewarded and promoted for doing less work. Many of us have been there: overlooked, undervalued, mansplained, excluded, undermined and made to feel invisible. A part of me couldn't understand it. I knew that I was visible in my workplace: being six foot one and Black there's no denying the fact that physically I stand out; I was known for doing a good job. However, I stood outside the dominant white culture. How could I be visible yet in actuality be invisible to the people that I thought knew and understood me? I was in plain sight yet unseen, masked by my background and discrimination; ghosted in plain sight. This is a recurring theme in my life as it is for all Black people.

The story of my demotion is not special and is commonplace for many Black people in working life, especially in the public sector where, in the UK, the number of Black and ethnic minority employees in leadership roles has remained static, at 1 per cent. Break this down further and Black women are twice as likely to be employed in insecure jobs compared to white women. The working realities for Black and white women are worlds apart, literally. Gender equality falls short for Black women. White women are generally seen; Black women are unseen and unheard.

In this chapter we will explore the different ways systemic racism and the intersections of oppression operate on the field of play and in the workplace, with a focus on Black women. In doing this we will reveal what leaders and individuals can do independently and collectively to ensure that everyone is seen. Oprah Winfrey powerfully summarized this point in her Harvard University 2013 commencement speech. Everyone, she said, wants to be validated and understood – even if they're President Obama or Beyoncé. When the camera stops rolling, everyone asks the same questions: 'Was that okay? Did you hear me? Did you see me? Did what I said mean anything to you?'

Standing at the intersecting crossroads of oppression

Centralizing the voices of Black women is not only important to me because I'm a Black woman but because it hardly ever happens. Black women experience discrimination differently because they stand at the crossroads of interlocking sets of oppression that make their individual experience multifaceted. This is known as intersectionality, a term coined by world-renowned academic and expert Professor Kimberlé Crenshaw, who uses it as a metaphor to understand the prism of multiple inequalities through which race inequality is viewed alongside other inequalities such as those based on gender, class, sexuality or immigration status; people are often subject to some or all of these, and each exacerbates the others. The intersections of oppression therefore impact on every facet of the lives of Black women – from our professional settings to the sports field. Serena Williams knows this well.

In 2018, at the US Tennis Open finals, one of the world's greatest tennis players of all time, Serena Williams, faced the double burden of the intersecting oppressions of racism and sexism and refused to be silenced. The Williams sisters have dominated a sport that is overwhelmingly white; they have battled and endured racial slurs, insults and outfit policing, and experienced unnecessary extra drug testing. Let's be crystal clear: the Williams sisters have a lot to be angry about. During the match which Serena Williams lost to Naomi Osaka, she was penalized for a series of code violations, including one for verbal abuse, after she confronted the umpire by calling him a thief. The violations were confusing for Serena, the spectators and millions of viewers, since the rules used by the umpire appeared to be arbitrarily applied. It was this that created the deep sense of injustice felt by Serena. It was clear that Serena had been held to different standards of behaviour compared to her fellow white male tennis players. The sexism was clear cut, the racism less so for white people, although for Black people it was plain to see. Those that feel, see. Shortly after, Rebecca Traister wrote in the New York magazine *The Cut* of how the umpire's censure of Williams had to be seen in the light of the inequalities she faced in terms of both her gender and race, just as with her recent pregnancy, where as a Black woman she had faced a higher risk of maternal mortality and postpartum complication.

Three days after the finals match on a bright sunny September day I went to the studios of *Channel 4 News* to be interviewed about Serena and my response to the situation. The interviewer was Fatima Manji. This made a difference: a talented and brilliant presenter who is a Muslim brown-skinned woman, Fatima automatically relaxed me; being in a collective If only of two people of difference enabled me to speak much more freely. That day I was choosing to highlight the invisibility of the dynamics of intersectional oppression of one of the world's most hyper-visible athletes while at the same time raising my own levels of visibility in the media and public eye.

By that time, male players including John McEnroe and James Blake had come forward to confirm that they have said much worse to chair umpires without being penalized. Tone policing is a common experience for all women and is more harshly applied to Black women, as Serena found out on that day when she was fined $17,000. I made this point in my interview with Fatima, who nodded along in agreement: 'There's nothing new to see here. This is the everyday experience of Black women. We can't be too emotive, too expressive, too angry. It just so happens that Serena's place of work is the tennis court.' I understood the strength and intensity of her response; I felt her anger because I feel it, too. Serena's anger is my anger and the justifiable anger and resistance of Black women. This force of rage serves to disrupt the pattern of oppressional harm. In her book *Eloquent Rage,* Brittney Cooper breaks this down and describes how watching Serena play is eloquent rage personified: her expressive, clear style and her exultant victories, she says, belong in a sense to all Black women.

In whatever way you choose to interpret the events of that match, the majority of Black woman can relate to Serena's reaction to the situation and recount a time when they have deeply wanted to respond in the same way. Racism plays itself out in the despicable ways stereotypical tropes are applied to Black women, something Serena is well versed in, and despite being one of the world's most famous tennis players, it is the stereotypes about Serena that make her hyper visible. Serena defies them through her excellence, of course. Her visibility is hidden by the stereotype of the Black woman – as angry, aggressive and strong. Serena is not viewed for the magnificent tennis player she is because to see her in her full humanity, the mainstream must address the oppression she faces as a Black woman. This is exactly why the tennis establishment holds her in what can only be described as sometimes disguised and at other times open contempt. This is in many ways the story of Black women in globalized society.

So, as it was for Serena so it is for Black women in the workplace: the experience of both racial and gender stereotypes further compounds the negative impact on the individual and intensifies the situation. We can't fight sexism without fighting racism. To tackle any form of inequality means tackling all forms of inequality whether that's fighting for LGBTQ+ rights the rights of people with disabilities, or those of women or Black communities.

Serena is an example of how competing oppressions impact Black women in the sports arena, and, like Serena, you, too, might be standing at the crossroads of various intersecting oppressions in any organization or team or group you're a part of. These oppressions are inextricably intertwined at a structural level in organizations, their different layers creating unequal outcomes for people from marginalized groups. For instance, in the UK both the ethnicity pay gap and the gender pay gap serve to doubly impact and bind Black women, yet where these pay gaps are reported, they are reported on separately. This division serves to erase Black women but also conceal their experiences. Their invisibility compounds the effects of racism in employment, negatively impacting their mental health and potentially causing them to leave their jobs. As the 2021 report of the UK Commission on Race and Ethnic Disparities highlights, Black, Asian and mixed-race women are more likely to experience common mental health disorders compared to the rest of the UK British adult population. In its 2020 *BME Women and Work* report the UK's Trades Union Congress highlights the higher numbers of BME women compared to both Black and White men and White women taking sick leave or leaving their job because of discrimination.

When I talk to company CEOs I stress the need for adopting approaches that take account of intersectionality because an understanding of how power and privilege are used to exclude or discriminate against different groups of women provides the starting point to increase their knowledge on how to best serve the needs of Black women in the workplace. Professor Kimberlé Crenshaw sums this up well, arguing that intersectionality is not just about identity but about how institutions use identity to exclude and privilege. In any industry, if the governance and leadership fail to understand the ways in which oppressions intersect, they fail to cater for the people they serve.

A word on the word. Why does this word 'intersectionality' even matter? It's become a fashionable term; I remember a time when it wasn't. I was once asked to write an article about intersectionality but not name it! The term has ben co-opted to capture broader protected characteristics, thereby diluting Kimberlé's original definition, which is unhelpful. To challenge and tackle any problem we need to be able to first define it. The term 'intersectionality' provides a language for us to do this. Language evolves, vocabulary changes ... but let's not waste any more time. If leaders are not with the programme, they need to get to it, quick time.

Tools for leaders

All UK institutions must reckon with the language of anti-racism, understand it and use it, just like they do with any new business or organizational terminology, and then enlist the help of experts if they need to.

Language matters because for some of us it can give voice to those unexpressed emotions that are a part of our experience in the world. A few years ago, I delivered a leadership workshop for women of colour working in sport. At the end of the three-hour session, two professional footballers of South-East Asian descent approached me excitedly, telling me how relieved they both were to have the terminology to finally explain their experiences both as players and media commentators. These two young women were happy to now have the words to define the racial trauma they had faced. Intuitively they had known what they were experiencing was wrong, but they didn't have the vocabulary to name it and then process it. Being able to process discrimination on an intellectual level helps those experiencing it to better understand it so they can recognize it and find ways to manage it. These women felt seen and therefore validated in a collective tribe of women who shared similar experiences.

Structural oppression

The statistics of UK racial disparities reveal the shocking levels of racism that exist in society. The negative experiences and life stories of UK Black communities, including my loved ones, are rooted in these narratives of entrenched racial injustices. Research, data and statistics take on a significant value and are vitally needed because they provide the evidence for so many who deny racism and the lived experiences of Black people that so often are up for debate and refuted.

The statistics provide the context. Black British Caribbean children are twice as likely to be permanently excluded from school as white pupils. Black British people are over four times more likely to be detained under the

Mental Health Act. The UK Black unemployment rate is double that of the White unemployment rate. We are nine times more likely to be stopped and searched by the police. Black families are five times more likely to be officially homeless than White families. Jobseekers with African- or Asian-sounding names must send up to 60 per cent more applications than White counterparts with equivalent CVs to get a positive response. The facts don't lie: the data is overwhelming regardless of the UK government's denial and rejection of the term 'institutional racism'.

So the scene is set? Not quite. As Layla Saad breaks down in her book *Me and White Supremacy*, the scaffolding of White supremacy, based on unearned privileges, power and protection, creates the environment for racial inequities to be permeated throughout every facet of life in overt and covert forms of racism, resulting in these racial disparities. But it is the system of White supremacy that enables and empowers white people to continually benefit from their privilege of being white. The system enables this privilege to perpetuate itself and is purposefully designed to keep those in privileged positions from fully knowing it and understanding it. I can now safely assert that expecting Black people to exist in a hostile system not created to benefit them is a false notion. I sincerely hope you agree.

We need to dismantle the old systems, create new ones, disrupt entrenched processes ... You name it, we need to do it ... *now*. From my experience there are senior leaders in organizations who are prepared to roll up their sleeves and undertake this kind of reform. It comes at a cost, and they often face serious backlash and organizational cultural resistance. This arises out of entrenched racism and patriarchy and causes efforts to quickly become fraught with tension and stalling. Tackling racism has to move beyond individual responsibility to a redistribution of resources and responsibilities so as to create new systems underpinned by a coalition of different voices.

Tools for leaders

One of the fundamental reasons there is a lack of meaningful progress in tackling structural racism is that the people who are part of the problem are the self-same people who are trying to solve the problem.

Whoa, big statement, right? Yes, and often it's not said as explicitly as that. One way – though not the *only* way, I hasten to add – to help redress racial inequities is to increase the ethnic and broader representation diversity of the workforce. Less than 10 per cent of British teachers are people of colour, which drops to less than 5 per cent for headteachers. There are just 7 per cent of police officers who are people of colour. A Business in the Community report found that Black people held just 1.5 per cent of the 3.7 million leadership positions across the UK's public and private sectors in 2019, compared with 1.4 per cent in 2014. The lack of Black leaders in business, industry and government across all senior positions in UK organizations results in a lack of visible Black role models. Let's unpick this together and look at ways to create a representative workforce through the lens of intersectionality and also how to increase the individual's visibility within this context. But first let me explain the power of the visible role model.

Representation and visibility – if you can see it, you can believe it

I have always loved Grace Jackson – no, not the musician Grace Jones, Grace Jackson the world-class 400m runner from Jamaica, who in the 1980s would glide so effortlessly around the track in all her glory. I wanted to be her every time I went out on the track. Kathy Cook was the British 400m runner of the time, but I just didn't relate to her in the same way I did to Grace. I modelled myself on Grace. I saw myself in her, a Black woman from the Caribbean. My family didn't have a lot of money back then, but my mum would buy us the cheap £3 seats at the Crystal Palace track, and on balmy summer London evenings we – my mum, my twin and I – would go and watch the likes of Merlene Ottey, Sonia Lannaman, Daley Thompson and Edwin Moses competing in all their full glory. Those cheap seats felt like the best seats in the house, as we sat among a sea of white faces having the time of our lives cheering on our favourite athletes, circling their names in the programmes and sprinting down the steep famous steps of the Crystal Palace Stadium in the hope we could get that elusive autograph from one of our idols. They were the best days ever. My lifelong love affair with athletics and sport started at Crystal Palace track. Years later I would be competing in the London Youth Games and inter counties meets on that very track where I saw my role models compete. The power of seeing someone who physically looks like you excel in their career inspires you to think that you, too, can achieve the same feats – that's what Grace Jackson did for me all those years ago.

Just as the power of the Black sports role model is immense so is that of high-profile leadership roles occupied by Black women in wider British society. This cannot be underestimated, as demonstrated by what has become known as the Kamala Harris effect. Kamala Harris shattered the glass ceiling of intersectional oppression when, in November 2020, she became the first Black woman of Jamaican and Asian descent to be elected the Vice President of the United States of America. Harris's impact is best captured by Bonnie Greer the American-British writer and cultural commentator, who in an article in the UK newspaper *The Telegraph* wrote how for too long '[t]he erasure of myself by society [had] made it so that I could not really see my own face in the mirror'. To truly see oneself, as a Black woman, is to acknowledge one's existence and 'for many black women that existence can be ambivalent; floating'. The election of Harris as 'the most powerful woman in American history … has empowered a generation of black girls to construct themselves, by their own rules'. She has become a prism through they can focus their abilities and dreams.

Tools for leaders

To create a diverse and representative workforce people from Black and marginalized identities need to see themselves represented throughout the organizational workforce, especially at a leadership level, as this illustrates that its possible for them to reach those same heights.

Some years ago, I was working with a large industrial company shortlisting candidates for a board position.

I was the only Black person on the recruitment panel completing the shortlisting and conducting the interviews. The organization wanted to improve the diversity of the board generally and in particular its ethnic representation, so I had been employed specifically to support it in this goal; I also helped devised the recruitment pack to reduce the impact of bias. There were 35 applications to review. I agreed with the shortlisting team on all applications to be shortlisted except for one – a Black woman who, I believed, met the criteria, even though none of the other five panellists agreed with me. As a Black woman I could see in between the lines of the application and how much the woman – we'll call her Toyin – had overcome to attain the senior positions she had held. Toyin, however, didn't have a high-profile name within the industry in the same way some of the other applicants had. I believed this added to her disadvantage in the eyes of the other panellists. I knew that Toyin's insights, experience and knowledge would be invaluable to the organization. When I raised this, my insights were met with a straightforward dismissal.

It's worth noting that there was one other Black woman who was already through to the interview stage, so my intuition told me that the shortlisting team felt as though they'd already met their diversity quota, and so didn't take my advice to include Toyin. I knew it was a mistake but, on this occasion, I was tired of raising my voice only for it not to be listened to (ironically, as I was being specifically employed for my race expertise) and I just couldn't come back with yet another rationale. I perhaps naively wanted my word to be trusted and that that word would be enough. I'd just come off another similar experience with another client so was mentally spent. I did, however, raise my concern in an email and copied in the administrator, and on interview day, to my surprise, Toyin was included and listed last on the schedule. I was secretly overjoyed; the other panellists were a bit bewildered and it was put down to an administrative error. I actually believe that the administrator trusted my word and had slotted her in. It came to the end of the day and the panellists were tired and expressed their annoyance that Toyin had made it through; everyone wanted to go home except me – I was excited about what was to come. I was right. Toyin blew everyone else out of the water and was by far the best candidate and was offered the role. This example shows the importance of having the right expertise and ethnic representation on recruitment panels. I was also grateful for that mysterious 'administrative error'.

Tools for leaders

If you are leading a recruitment process and working with a Black or Brown people expert, believe them when they talk, afford them the luxury of the benefit of the doubt, understand their intuition and that things you cannot see or understand matter. Their lived experience is in their gift to you, so believe them the first time round!

If the system is rigged not to see you, in the way it was for Toyin, then to play catch up you are forced into taking matters into your own hands. Being visible in your professional life is about being recognized and credited for your work both when you're in the room and outside of the room. Your personal responsibility must start with a deep understanding of who you are, your talents, strengths and areas for development. Visibility is about owning your story and being able to articulate and demonstrate your achievements for yourself and others. Having visibility with no influence can take you only so far, and sometimes we need others to help us see ourselves. Therefore, building and nurturing new and old relationships by growing a community of champions who advocate for you when you're not in the room can be a gamechanger. This can come in the form of mentors, peers and sponsors who can be part of your very own 'hype' team, introducing you to new networks, audiences and opportunities aligned to your interests, skillset and identity. Sponsorship and mentoring programmes internally or externally to the organization you work for can also be of benefit to increasing your profile.

These kinds of programmes can be a driver to increase the representation and visibility of Black and marginalized groups and build a pipeline to senior positions in organizations. Sponsors must understand their role in supporting the individual in the fullness of their various identities, spending time learning and understanding the unique and additional barriers the individual experiences in professional life. This will help to create a deeper connection and a trusting relationship. When this works well the sponsor can create more meaningful and relatable opportunities that support the professional and personal growth of the individual. Through this process the sponsor will learn first-hand the real-life impact of racism and intersectional oppression, and how their organizational culture perpetuates it or not. Good practice can also include policies such as creating work shadowing opportunities, sharing reports from senior board meetings, and asking mentees what decisions they would take. This kind of activity exposes mentees to new areas of work and expands their network. Organizations must be mindful of the power dynamic at play; it's about creating bespoke and nuanced programmes of support where the sponsor is fully aware of the mentee's talents and specific experiences and where full reciprocity of equity and empathy is built into the relationship. As a Black person it can at times be a challenge to find a sponsor who is prepared to support your journey. This why it is critical to work in an environment open to these kinds of programmes with senior leaders who have fully bought into identifying, creating and supporting Black talent.

Tools of resistance

Identify your champions and enlist their active support in enhancing and accelerating your career.

Even if we have our own board of sponsors and champions, it's nevertheless up to us to be our own biggest cheerleader. This is not an entirely comfortable experience for some people, but it is your personal responsibility: if you're not prepared to back yourself, how can you possibly expect others to? Hang tight because in Chapter 4 I share how we can find ways to overcome self-doubt by learning from some of the best sportspeople.

One strategy that can help anyone is to find opportunities outside of work to be recognized for your achievements and contributions in a safe space. This is known as the 'awards landscape'. This is specifically true for Black women. In 2016 I won the PRECIOUS Award for women of colour in the Outstanding Woman in Sport category. This award was founded by the extraordinary Foluke Akinlose MBE and is one of the biggest events in the UK's business calendar, celebrating the achievements of women of colour in business, leadership and work. To be truly seen for all my unseen work was immensely powerful for me. I felt valued for my contribution to making a difference for others, and at the same time it raised my profile, increasing my visibility and showcasing my work as an individual changemaker.

Awards and recognition play a role in uncovering and revealing new stories of people from marginalized identities who are routinely undervalued, underserved and often not celebrated because they belong to a minority group and as such their efforts go unseen. The power of one award for one individual can have a big effect on their community. When I won the PRECIOUS Award women in my network were inspired by the accolade and felt as if, through their connection to me, that they had partly won, too. When you deeply and truly understand that your successes are not yours alone, that they belong to the ancestral pride to those who have come before you and for those who will come after you, it liberates you to step into your light. This is something I always mention in my panel talks to organizational leaders: when Black women win awards external to their organizations it's important to celebrate, acknowledge and share this success internally with the staff workforce. This can sometimes result in the organizations viewing Black women's skills in a new light.

> **Tools of resistance**
>
> You never know whom you're inspiring, so it's a responsibility of those of us from minority groups to share success stories, from big awards to everyday moments of triumph.

Awards and recognition offer external validation, but they are no substitute for seeing and valuing yourself. We have to determine our own value and define this for ourselves as well. Seeking validation from people and organizations that have limited expectations of you is a falsehood and detrimental to your wellbeing. Therein lies the trap for Black people or other people from marginalized identities who may be tempted to change to fit in – and be seen to fit in – with a homogenized institutional culture – in short, to try to be what they are not to attain approval and recognition in a culture that is constructed not to see them. Own your success by understanding it and reminding yourself about the bigger and smaller achievements that make up your life tapestry.

Excellence exceptionalism versus hyper-(in)visibility

For some people, increasing your visibility can come with dangers. Take LeBron James, Serena Williams, Usain Bolt, Simone Biles, Nicola Adams, Lewis Hamilton, Dina Asha-Smith, Tiger Woods. These are athletes and superstars who have unquestionably dominated their sports, achieving global success and stardom. Yet Black athletes are still living a life of double consciousness, a concept coined in 1903 by civil rights leader and theorist W. E. B. Du Bois to refer to having two social identities. This is a very relevant concept in present-day global society and can be linked to the ways in which some Black people feel the need to code-switch in order to fit into spaces where white people are the majority. Professor Ben Carrington has highlighted the ways in which Black athletes are forced into seeing themselves through a racialized lens, where brands portray Black athletes as physically superhuman yet intellectually inferior. Black athletes are viewed merely for their physical prowess based on racial myths and stereotypes. This has a negative impact on the consciousness of the Black athlete who views her- or himself outside of their own identity through two social identities, one of their choosing and one enforced.

Former sprinter queen and now leading sports broadcaster Jeanette Kwakye articulates another facet of the Black athlete's social identities when she wrote that is like being both 'the nation's sweetheart' and 'a pariah', viewed as talented and patriotic as long as you don't take a step out of turn. And in an interview in *Vogue* magazine in 2020, British heptathlete Katrina Johnson-Thompson gave a moving account of her experience of racism and also pointed to what happened to the Black England footballer Marcus Rashford who was lionized for his campaign to end child hunger during the COVID-19 crisis, only to be called 'Daniel' by the British Secretary for Health and Social Care, who made no effort to disguise his reluctance to mention him at all. The complexity and contradictions of hypervisibility overlayed with racism is a heavy burden for the Black athlete, just as it is for other prominent Black people in British society.

Sir Trevor McDonald (TV newsreader and journalist), Karen Blackett (one of the UK's most senior Black woman in the advertising media industry), Sharon White (managing director of John Lewis, one of the UK's leading department stores), the rapper Stormzy and the philanthropist Sir Ken Olisa are all incredibly successful Black individuals at the top of their fields, yet, despite titles, accolades, achievements, qualifications, awards and appearing on illustrious Black British lists, they will always face discrimination at some level. Much like superstar athletes, their very success obscures the fullness of their Black identities, which remains unacknowledged by the mainstream white public. It is this white perspective that leads England footballer Raheem Sterling to be appreciated on the pitch when he is scoring stunning goals but drowned out by boos of dissent and ignorance when he takes a knee to protest against racism. In other words, what some white people are really saying is that they revel in, absolutely see, want and value a Black person's sporting excellence but don't want to see them in their humanity as a Black person because otherwise they would have to accept and confront their own racism. We saw this vividly at the 2020 Euros football tournament when the England team took the knee before each match. We saw it when, after they lost to penalties in the final, the Black players responded publicly to the vicious racism they received.

Black super achievers are keenly aware of these external dynamics, and this adds to the pressure of retaining their position of excellence. They all know how difficult it is to stay at the top of their chosen field, whether that's in the boardroom, classroom or out on the pitch or court. Being successful, making progress, retaining status and creating opportunities for others to follow are all big challenges when you're in the minority and you're confronted by spaces that by default exclude you. These hyper-visible Black stars play an important role in aspiring Black people to be their own versions of excellence.

In 2018 I was lucky enough to secure a ticket to hear former first lady of the US Michelle Obama speak at the Southbank Centre during her visit to London. I'll never forget queuing up to buy tickets. It was stressful as we were competing with thousands of people online, such was the desire in the Black community and others to get tickets. Later that day I had to give a talk at the Baton Awards for women of colour hosted in the Houses of Parliament. and began my speech by sharing that I had secured my tickets, to be met with mass exclamations of congratulation and boos of jealousy.

The night came and the auditorium was filled with important dignitaries, members of the public and 200 schoolgirls form across London. It was an inspirational, honest, funny and utterly compelling conversation between Michelle and the writer Chimamanda Ngozi Adichie. The atmosphere was exhilarating and celebratory. Michelle's energy and direct way of speaking her truths and sharing life lessons packed full of wisdom resonated deeply with the audience; everyone could find something to relate to. I particularly loved seeing the young people listening so intently to Michelle's special wisdom. This opportunity to see and listen to Michelle, who embodies everything that inspires me, will stay with me for ever. I share her life lessons in the seminars and coaching I do today. That's the power of the relatable role model.

When you hear the stories of successful people who have suffered from the same voices of self-doubt as you do and have come from similar backgrounds, something special happens and you see that you are not alone in your day-to-day challenges. I've also been privileged enough to be on panels alongside some exceptionally inspiring people. There is power in this kind of connection, and it helps build individual and collective resilience.

Tools of resistance

Hearing other people's stories helps you to understand your world through their world. Many environments don't nurture the success or interests of Black people, so being in spaces where experiences of Black success are articulated is of high value.

We've covered a lot of the track in this chapter – from how and why intersectional oppression operates to the individual ways in which we can all take responsibility for how we share our own stories. Wherever you find yourselves in your relationship with visibility, be it proudly standing in your truths, or trying to find firmer ground in the face of oppression, we all have access to our inner resilience and sense of identity that enables us to take up space as individual leaders in our own right. In Chapter 3 we will explore how to do this authentically and powerfully by redefining your personal and professional boundaries for success.

We have also seen that organizational leaders must do better and create the interventions and programmes that increase the visibility of Black success in the workforce. It will only be after this is achieved that we will be all seen, heard and understood. As we close out this chapter, as is often the way in life, we come full circle as I repeat Oprah's words with which I began, in the hope that your answer is a resounding (or even uncertain) 'yes' – 'Was that okay? Did you hear me? Did you see me? Did what I said mean anything to you?'

Real wins

- To redress racial inequities, organizational leaders must undertake a forensic examination of every part of their ecosystem identifying the places where structural racism can lead to unfair decisions and racial and gender inequities.

- Organizations must reform recruitment processes based on understanding representation and intersectional oppression.

- Get crystal clear on your strengths and learn how to powerfully articulate them to increase your visibility.

- Shine your light by owning your achievements and sharing your big and small successes far and wide: you never know whom you're inspiring and the impact that inspiration can have.

Redefining the boundaries

A young man excitedly raised his hand, waving at me at the same time, keen for me to see him first. I picked him out and he asked, 'How many children do you have, Miss, and are you married?' I was perplexed. I'd just finished giving a talk to around 400 fifteen-year-old students at an inner-city London school. My brief had been to give an inspirational speech sharing tips for success as the students embarked on their most important school year yet, of examinations and preparing for their next steps. 'None and no!' I said while silently responding in my head: 'Seriously?! After everything I've just said for the last 30 minutes, that's your first question.' I'm not sure why I was surprised in all honesty – after all, it's a reaction I've often had to face.

I scrambled around in the perimenopausal folders of files in my head knowing that my answer had to be easily understood and make an impact. I lowered and quietened my voice and slowed the pace of my words down (a speaking technique for professional speakers to get your words to connect deeply with your audience). 'I write my own story I've never fitted into these conventional, very gendered boxes of expectations.' I paused and saw – and felt – the nods of the young women sitting in the sports hall. I smiled at a few of them almost conspiratorially. I continued: 'We can and should define our own boxes. I've often been the youngest, the only Black woman and the boss. I now have an unconventional job; one I've written the job description for based on my passions and I make my own money. Having or not having children or being married does not define me as a woman. My encouragement to all of you today is to write your own story, not one that has to keep up with somebody else's or what society expects of you.'

My answer wasn't what my questioner had expected, and he looked a bit bewildered. I moved on to the next question. The unfortunate fact is that this question is a common one for women, and there's a further assumption that because on the face of it I have a successful career that this is my focus as opposed to being married with a family. Whether this is truth or not is not the point. It happens routinely. Even when I shared the news of my book deal with my friends and people in my network, and I started with the line 'I've got big news …' the common joking response was 'Are you pregnant or getting married, Michelle? It's about time.' This is a joke based on patriarchy, so I can't find the humour in it. Nonconformity is one of the themes of my life. I clearly don't fit into any boxes, never have and never will. I thrive outside of them. Quite literally at times. It was only in 2001 that 'mixed' appeared on the UK census forms, a word that might begin to describe my identity as a Black woman of Guyanese and English mixed heritage. Even so, I never ticked that box but always ticked Black instead, as that's how I see myself politically and that's the identity that has negatively impacted and continues to impact my life chances.

Now as the managing director of my own company, people are forever asking me, 'Who are you? Who do you work for?', assuming I'm an associate for a large firm or work for a sports organization. My whole career and the roles I've had to some extent have afforded me latitude to be unconventional. Nonconformity and unconventionality are the dominant notes of my current career. I fit in between the spaces and that's where I actually belong, and I find my tribe of fellow people along the way. I set my agenda, control my narrative, author my own content, and the characters I play are ones of my choosing.

Being judged, labelled or categorized in a way that doesn't reflect your individual identify can impact your career progression. Adapting a mindset which resists and rejects such labels, and redefining our own boundaries, enables us to realize our own definition of personal and professional success.

Debunking the myth of the imposter syndrome

Negative stereotypes that infect mainstream public consciousness can dangerously impact your self-perception. This social conditioning negatively affects your levels of confidence, self-esteem and self-belief. It is critical that we find ways to reject such toxic marginalization.

One such term is the problematic phrase 'imposter syndrome', which was first coined by clinical psychologists Pauline Clance and Suzanne Imes in 1978 to describe a pattern of behaviour where people doubt their accomplishments and have a persistent, often internalized fear of being exposed as a fraud. In recent years imposter syndrome has become a label used by many people to describe experiences of self-doubt – the feeling of not being worthy of accolades or achievements and one day being found out to be an imposter. But labels don't apply to all people equally, and in this case imposter syndrome is predominantly used to perpetuate the myth that women lack confidence. It has become a convenient justification for explaining why women's careers don't progress and for explaining the lack of a pipeline of women, and especially Black women, reaching senior jobs in organizations. This places the blame always on the individual rather than on the system which is what creates imposter syndrome. Punishing white women for lacking confidence and one step further for Black women for showing too much of it. One thing is clear all women suffer under this term.

As human beings we all universally experience moments of self-doubt and lack confidence at different times in our lives. It's the human condition: we are not static and so our confidence ebbs and flows. There are, of course, people who generally lack confidence as part of their personality traits and characteristics. Imposter syndrome has hijacked these feelings of self-doubt, especially for women in the workplace. In an article in the *Harvard Business Review*

Ruchika Tulshyan and Jodi-Ann Burey break this down further, explaining how white men's feelings of doubt usually abate through their careers, because they are supported by accessible role models and because their competencies and intelligence are rarely questioned as they are validated over time; having neither of these advantages, women experience exactly the opposite.

Imposter syndrome, properly understood, runs deeper than feelings of self-doubt; it is about the internalization of these feelings based on societal norms. It is this aspect of imposter syndrome that is most dangerous for Black people. It is this internalization as part of the impact of racism, sexism and structural inequalities which causes a lack of confidence, self-doubt and anxiety, firmly and subliminally reminding Black people of their lack of power in Western societies. The conventional use of the term 'imposter syndrome' serves the dominant culture, which is white, male, straight and cisgender. It is unseeing of the intersectional oppression and marginalization which impacts the career trajectory and progression of people from marginalized groups.

When I met with her to discuss this issue, author and activist Nova Reid asserted: 'Imposter syndrome is never feeling like you belong, which is often rooted in racism.' Imposter syndrome for Black people, and Black women especially, is of no consequence in the face of intersectional oppression. Racism in Western societies creates negative stereotypes of Black people which can cause Black people to question their own skills and expertise, without unhelpful terms such as imposter syndrome further reinforcing this. It is the culture of exclusion that causes people to feel like they don't belong, rather than a lack of confidence.

Tools of resistance

The self-awareness work is in the rewriting of these internal negative scripts or stories so they become more empowering, enabling us to boldly craft out new roles and develop a new, sustaining and healthy belief system.

The Stanford psychologist Claude Steele asserts that there is a stereotype threat where stereotypes can undermine the performance of the people they target and reduce the performance of many different groups. That is to say that just being aware of the dominant culture's negative stereotypes of your identity group can adversely affect the performance of that group. Stories which are largely based on negative societal labels can become life-limiting beliefs. This relates to everyone who is not part of the main culture of their professional environment. Taking responsibility for your own life is about powerfully redefining the often negative stories you keep telling and retelling yourself.

Checking the evidence of our lives

Having a strong sense of self is an important foundation for moments of self-doubt on the journey towards your own definition of personal and professional success. To illustrate this, let me tell you a story.

I was sitting on the edge of the hotel bed on the verge of tears. I was in Malaysia on a trip organized by the UK government and a national sports charity with the brief to develop a school's exchange project. I was there with a teacher from another British school, and we had met with staff from the schools we had been paired with, in order to gather intelligence for the design of an innovative physical activity intervention for young people in both UK and Malaysian schools. Our programmes had to be different from each other because our schools had very contrasting demographics. I came up with an innovative project idea which involved a multi-agency approach working with health professionals, a local sports club, parents and the school PE department. I shared my idea excitedly and openly with the other teacher. This turned out to be a huge mistake. He did something that at the time I couldn't quite believe. At the daily update meeting with the team, he announced his proposal – which I quickly realized was exactly my idea. It was such a blatant theft of my creative work and labour I was stunned into silence. I knew, too, that if I wasn't silent, I would be taking on a potential fight given this teacher's personality type. I could see the intellectual verbal gymnastics I'd have to go through, and I didn't have the brain space or emotional energy for it. As a young teacher in a new country I already felt somewhat out of my depth, in truth. Hence my silence. I'd been creatively pickpocketed! I was left with no other choice but to come up with a new idea.

My time was running out, and I needed to come up with a new project sharpish. I'd been specially selected to be a part of this national programme, and my school was proud of me and the students couldn't wait to be involved in whatever project I came up with because they would get to travel to Malaysia, which, for those young people, was massive. Because of the intergenerational worklessness in their families, some of them had hardly ever left their local community, let alone travelled abroad. There was a lot riding on my creativity juices in that moment. I could feel the start of a panic attack coming on. I took a few deep breaths and did what I always do in moments of stress: I telephoned my twin sister, Françoise, in the hope that this would inspire me and kick-start my imagination. She recounted my past projects but it was to no avail.

Then the hotel phone rang. It was my dad; my sister had lovingly grassed me up and had called him. After listening patiently as I moaned about Andrew having stolen my idea, in his no-nonsense style Dad said, 'Michelle, You're from the Walworth Road! Have you forgotten who you are? You've survived the rough, tough streets of South London; how hard can this problem be?' In that moment my dad reminded me of who I was, reaffirming my identity and heritage and that we'd survived far worse than my current predicament. I laughed, and my frustration eased and the stress disappeared. Reflecting on the evidence of my life before that point had helped me and provided much needed perspective.

In our moments of self-doubt, checking the evidence of our previous achievements and success reminds us that we've overcome past challenges. Fact-checking success builds the belief that it can be repeated. It is possible to confront internalized stereotypes objectively through this evidence checking. Speaking with one of your champions, a member of your tribe or family, or a trusted advisor, can help remind you of your strengths and who you are in the world and serve to reaffirm your identity and cultural capital. My sister had provided me with the evidence of my previous successful projects and my dad had reminded me of my rich heritage. After that conversation with my dad I felt reassured and relaxed and trusted that the ideas would emerge, and it would all work out ... and, of course, it did. I came up with an even better project to everyone's delight – except the ideas thief's, that is.

Tools of resistance

Checking the evidence of past achievements and tuning into the power of your identity and heritage can help break the confidence deadlock in moments of stress.

What I absolutely don't want to do in my work is place the blame on the shoulders of the victim because this is not where the blame lies, contrary to the concept of the imposter syndrome and Sheryl Sandberg's *Lean In* tips – these concepts and subsequent self-help principles simply don't stack up for Black women and Black people generally because we don't possess the access codes to privilege in the same way white people do. It's these access codes that we will turn to next.

How to break the deadlock: do you have the access code?

There are times when self-belief and confidence are not enough. Cracking open the deadlock of oppression can be almost impenetrable for Black people and those from other marginalized identities, even for those who might be best placed to challenge it.

Kwame – not his real name, I hasten to add – was a well-respected HR professional and had joined a large organization to help deliver equality training to hundreds of employees and other organizations. For the first three months Kwame was happy in his role. Soon, a new colleague, Brian (again, not his real name), joined the team. Brian, who was white, had fewer qualifications than Kwame and was working at the same level as him, which Kwame thought was odd, but he didn't pay much attention to it at first as he was too busy inducting Brian into his new role. Brian soon confided in Kwame that he didn't have an HR equalities background and had heard about the role because he knew the manager through the chess club his dad was a member of. As a Black man and equalities expert, Kwame was well versed in the ways in which nepotism operates, giving white people access to employment opportunities. Then, through an email mistakenly sent to him, Kwame learned that Brian was being paid a higher salary than he was. Kwame addressed this with his manager, and although the manager was sympathetic, their response centred on the fact that budget pressures meant that there was no funding to redress pay inequities and no action was taken to resolve the situation. Kwame was placed in what he felt was an untenable position; a huge part of his role was about equity and inclusion and here he was in his own organization facing discrimination. He chose to stand in his values and resigned. Left with racial battle fatigue, he had to seek therapy to help him process all that had happened.

Across industries, in much the same way as Kwame, Black people lack the access codes of privilege to access leadership positions, and this is no different for athletes post-retirement. In English football, 33 per cent of players on the pitch are from a Black or Asian background. Given this statistic you would expect retired players to progress into management and coaching roles, yet there are only five Black football managers. The systemic racism embedded into the fabric of English football negatively impacts the opportunities for people from Black and Asian backgrounds to access coaching, administration and leadership roles in the game. In the United States the picture is just as bleak. There are 32 NFL teams and roughly 70 per cent of players are Black, yet at the start of the 2020 NFL season there were just three Black head coaches and two Black general managers. This despite the Rooney Rule, which requires teams hiring a head coach to interview at least one person of colour.

Benny Bonsu and Samantha Johnson are both highly talented British sports broadcasters and journalists, yet despite qualifications and a decade of experience, they have struggled to land the big jobs and be recognized for their accomplishments and talents in the UK. These accomplished women secured high-profile roles outside the UK so they could feel valued and recognized for their contributions. Samantha is now the Chief Sports Anchor and journalist at TRT World in Turkey and host at FIFA, while Benny is is the Director of Daily Content for the International Olympic Committee based in Spain. Who knows how long they would have had to wait for their big breaks in the UK? In speaking to them during the writing of this book, they spoke openly about feeling that they would never have never achieved such success in the UK. Despite being highly talented, they were told that their faces didn't fit; in Samantha's case, she was even given the excuse that she didn't have enough sparkle compared to her white peers. It's no surprise that they have now gained the respect of their British industry peers and executives in new ways. Why do our best talents have to leave to ultimately be seen in their own countries of origin?

These talented people with the clear potential to reach the top of their profession couldn't overcome the inherently racially biased recruitment processes of the media and sports industries so had to adapt and adjust their plans to create and seek other opportunities. This demonstrates the lived experience of Black people unable to access spaces of privilege where decisions are made or entrance is gained to the networks, roundtables, invitation-only dinners and the social spaces where the key relationships are developed. Black people do not hold the keys or passwords to the opportunities of privilege that white people do.

Perhaps they should have taken up golf! The golf course is well known as the place to make business deals in British society. Tunji Akintokun MBE did just this. At the tender age of 22 Tunji received some advice from his mentor, a white man who told him to take up golf. Tunji became a proficient golfer and along the way networked business opportunities which, he feels, have accelerated his career. He is now one of the senior directors at Pricewaterhouse-Coopers UK and holds a list of impressive non-executive board roles and is a massive advocate for equality. We can't all take up golf, though! The codes or privilege need to be cracked. Some of these 'codes' are straightforward capital letters and easier to crack, but the majority are at least eight characters including a number and symbol, because they are entirely dependent on organizational context.

It's risky for Black people to speak out about the racism they feel and are facing because of the potential negative consequences on their career – termed 'career retribution' – and increased difficulty of securing future employment. The acclaimed historian David Olusoga MBE captured this in his address to the Edinburgh Television Festival in August 2020 when he said, 'The more you speak out the more unemployable you become.' When you can't break the code, then you have to find an entirely different key-pad. Creating access to opportunity and equity is the business of inclusive leadership and high-performing teams.

I want us to reimagine a world where we could get rid of the need for a pin pad for the access code altogether. I like to think the majority of people do want a world where the values of respect and opportunity are available to everyone. They are well-intentioned, good people who happen to be operating in bad systems.

Tools for leaders

The solution lies in creating inclusive and safe environments which are resilient to cognitive dissonance. To tackle the inherent racial biases that negatively impact recruitment processes, talent identification, career progression, and recognizing and valuing difference, organizations must invest heavily in their people's personal and professional growth to enable employees to embark on the journey of learning to tackle their own forms of racism and inherent biases.

I absolutely do not mean one-off diversity and unconscious bias training, which are proven not to work, but ongoing deep leadership development programmes of exploration and support. This is not about creating environments where everything is rosy; it's about creating spaces where it is safe to be different; where employees are able to talk about racism, and where opposing views and tensions can still exist and be held in a safe space.

Invariably, this will create conflict and cognitive dissonance. However, it is possible to create the environment that can hold this tension and offer a mutually safe space for people to make mistakes, make atonement and move on. Often through fear and not wanting to have difficult conversations people can make this more complex than it needs to be. This requires experienced managers and employees who are committed to managing difference both at the organizational and individual level. I've been in teams where the emotional and intellectual power is not held by the senior leaders but by the emotionally intelligent entry-level employee who is skilfully and sensitively able to work within a team dynamic that holds opposing views. This is why comprehensive high-quality leadership development programmes are needed. Quality leadership development includes creating safe spaces for inclusive practice. These are the kinds of training interventions that can create cultural shifts, where teams of people are intentional about changing structures to enable Black talent to be seen and nurtured to move beyond the falsehoods of organizational diversity and inclusion statements full of empty promises and rhetoric.

When I give seminars to companies, I often assert that when Black people or those from other marginalized identities do use their voices, it is essential they are listened to and, above all, heard and not dismissed. Active listening from organizational leaders is important in understanding the dynamics and impact of racism, especially given that for decades organizations have struggled to meaningfully engage with issues of race and ethnicity and often come from a place of fear, ignorance and self-proclaimed perceived uncertainty. Leading antiracism academic scholar Professor Ibram X. Kendi argues that the heart of racism is denial, and that no change is possible unless that denial is dismantled.

Tools for leaders

Creating safe spaces for developing truth and reconciliation processes to understand the honest experiences of Black people will help to create new opportunities to unravel, unlearn and learn new antiracism ways of being.

If organizational leaders decided to take on the work of dismantling systemic racism in a similar way to any other company-wide strategic objective, they would be making a good start. A company can redefine itself when it has to implement a new business-wide IT system, through company-wide interventions, strategic planning, allocating funds, commissioning external experts, training the workforce and undertaking change management processes. In a similar way, by applying resources to tackling racism, through planning, funding, employing experts and installing a commitment to challenge it wherever it exists, leaders can open the door to positive change at an organizational level.

It is adopting this kind of approach which will start to create antiracism outcomes. One of the issues faced by large institutions in tackling antiracism work is the notion that it's more difficult than any other business objective because the effort is focused on changing people's attitudes. The problem with this is that attitudinal change takes time, and this can then slow down progress and much needed action. A focus on creating antiracist outcomes and changing behaviours must come first, and although it's not a neat and tidy process, attitudinal change may well have to play catch-up.

As part of Black History Month events in October 2020, I was interviewed on a UK Sport podcast alongside Sport England Board member Chris Grant. The interview was with the Chair of UK Sport and GB's most decorated Olympic rower, Dame Katherine Grainger. I was asked what happens to those people in organizations who don't get on board with new ways of working when antiracism practice is implemented. I was unapologetic and unequivocal in my response: 'It is our responsibility to create working cultures where everyone can succeed, and being transparent about the acceptable antiracist behaviours that the company wants to represent is key. If this makes some employees uncomfortable, then they should leave because they are not the right employees for the organization. There is no place for those people working in British sport. So, I'd say a hearty goodbye.' By their very nature, inclusive environments create a culture where there is a zero tolerance for racism and other forms of oppression. This then becomes an untenable space for people who display racist and bias behaviours, resulting in them exiting that culture.

For Black people there's no escape from experiencing racism. For some they don't recognize it as part of their Black experience. I've sat in audiences and on panels where Black people, women and people from minority groups have categorically refuted that they have experienced any kind of oppression. They may not have experienced overt oppression, but by the mere fact of their identity their lives are affected by covert oppression. The issue with expressing this is that it can be problematic to rehearse in front of audiences because it is used by some people as an excuse to not do the work of tackling racism.

A Black, highly sought-after cultural commentator and race expert was once speaking to a large group of business administrators. The audience was made up of mainly white men with one sole Black man in attendance. It was a tense affair, and the audience was very defensive and resistant to the commentator's antiracist viewpoints. During the Q&A the only Black man in the audience said that he didn't agree with the speaker's views as he had never experienced racism in that organization. This is one of the most damaging and pernicious parts of racism because it undermines and oppresses Black people all at the same time, so that they don't realize it's happening to them. He had become culturalized to the institutional racism in his organization. In denouncing racism this person legitimized white people's defensiveness and maintained the status quo and in so doing added to his own oppression. Whenever I hear and witness this internalized racism it's a stark reminder of how deep the wounds of oppression cut and the need for compassion all round. Black people can be victims of internalized racism, but the way it manifests is different for different people

Black people, as with any other ethnic group, are all at different stages of consciousness when it comes to issues of race. Often, this is linked to age and lived experience. This is true for some of the Black athletes I have mentored. I've seen them grow in their consciousness, and as a consequence their thinking has changed as they become more knowledgeable and wiser to the environments and the ways in which their words can be manipulated in unhelpful ways in the media or on the platforms they use. It is part of the complexity of the struggle for Black people to not only resist racial oppression and injustice but also to recognize the oppressive values which have been forced upon us in such a way that we unknowingly internalize them. The dynamic of racism is so sophisticated it can make you question if you are contributing to it in some way. This happens to some degree to all marginalized groups, such are the intricacies and toxicity of oppression that robs humankind of its humanity.

Perhaps it is evidence of the emotional burden that writing this book has placed on me that I needed to regroup after writing this part. It felt a bit like how I used to after killer sessions made up of back-to-back 300m runs!

Redefining success

As things stand, when you hit the glass ceilings of oppression, dislike, distrust and envy, you have no other choice but to redefine your vision of success. It's not going to be that direct ladder to promotion you envisaged and so you have to get creative and, as unjust as it is, design a new route. That might be getting a new job, taking a sideways position in your company, going freelance, developing a new business, identifying an external mentor or sponsor, or reinventing yourself in an existing role. Developing your personal and professional strategy for success is a critical tool in your personal development and career progression. Compartmentalizing success into personal and professional desires is the first step in designing a 'life on purpose'.

Tools of resistance

Intentionally and consciously clarifying your limiting beliefs and learning how to recognize oppressional barriers, while being realistic about your likely career trajectory, is critical. With clarity about what you want in your life, you can move from merely surviving to thriving.

Developing daily wellbeing practices can be effective in helping you to achieve this. I've seen miraculous results in the lives of people I've coached and mentored when they've adopted some very simple activities. Successful people know that in order to be successful they have to be still. By quietening the mind, we can create distance between our thoughts, which helps us to find those moments of clarity to help craft our life plans. We can achieve this through meditation, prayer, mindfulness, spiritual practice, play, physical activity, or any activity we become completely immersed in. There's ample research that demonstrates the positive benefits of physical activity to boost our mental health, of course. As a netball player, without fail my only intention at a Saturday morning match is to prevent the ball from going into the net with my six-foot-one stretch. It is a completely exhilarating and at the same time liberating being in the zone; I'm completely detached from anything else in my life.

Through these practices and activities we can become more grounded with a deeper sense of what it is we want in our lives despite the pressure of societal conventions. By becoming clear about what will bring us more fulfilment we become clear about what we *don't* want in our lives, which can become the first step in redefining our versions of success. It is this redefinition that can create individual personal and professional transformation. Creating your own self-imposed boundaries enables you to say 'no' to what might superficially appear to be very exciting projects but which in reality don't align to your strategic life plan and desires. This redefinition helps you to spot the genuine opportunities when they appear. When we experience any kind of oppression, we can then be guided by our own internal satellite navigation system based on our strategic life plans and values. This makes it easier to decide on which oppression battles to fight and when. Sometimes, especially in the talks I give, I can be in full-on activist warrior mode, and at other times I choose to conserve my 'resistance fuel', instead, and operate at a lower (yet still-impactful) frequency, allowing resilience refuelling to take place so I'm ready to take on the next big life challenges.

> **Tools of resistance**
>
> Having the courage to follow your own internal satellite navigation system is where the true power lies.

Living outside boundaries

Over a lovely dinner one winter's evening, a friend and mentor said, 'You know, Michelle you should go for more CEO roles.' I smiled pleasantly, but internally I sighed because I knew being a CEO wasn't for me. He continued: 'People will look at you differently, it will look great on your CV and you'll get more respect. It will really help you, I just know it.' This advice was well intended. Other people's versions of success for you can often have a big impact on the career choices we make and take. Yet the story of my life and identity have and always been nonconformist so it's important to me to follow my own beat. Society views CEOs as having powerful and visible roles, but being the CEO of your life is about powerfully making decisions that work best for your own agenda and nobody else's.

Reviewing and redefining your version of success is an ongoing process which can be life-changing at pivotal transition points in your life. This happened to me when I worked as a senior leader in the public sector. I'd become frustrated and bored, I didn't see any career progression I was passionate about and was becoming less and less motivated. I was searching for more meaning in my life. Initially, I registered with a recruitment company, which, given my existing senior leadership role, organized meetings for me with top sports brands, companies and charities, including

CEO roles. This would have been the natural next step in my career, and yet I was completely underwhelmed by the prospect of a CEO-type role. When I carefully considered the job specifications, I realized that I was already working in that capacity in my current position without the CEO title and yet still with the same kinds of leadership responsibilities. I decided to stay put and reinvent parts of my work portfolio in a way more aligned to my passions. I read Bob Buford's book *Half Time*, which introduced me to the concept of the 'percentage effort'. If you've been working at something for a decade, you've pretty well mastered it and so you can afford to adjust your work rate and percentage effort. I realized I could probably work at half speed and still achieve the same results for my employer. This was what I call a defining 'real win' moment. I consciously turned down my percentage efforts in my role and created thinking space in my head for my next career chapter. In time, I reduced my hours to part-time, eventually left and crafted a new career plan by redesigning, reimagining and redefining my version of success.

Tools of resistance

Organizations have strategic plans outlining objectives, goals, milestones, KPIs, dates and so on which include our roles and responsibilities as a part of their team. Yet many of us don't apply the same kind of strategy to our own lives – we don't afford ourselves the opportunity of figuring out what success looks like for us and how we can work towards it, even just loosely – for example 'I'd like to own my own property, run a marathon, achieve a qualification in five years' time ...'

As a consultant I have a diverse career portfolio working for different clients, from the London Mayor's office to the Commonwealth Games Federation. Despite my success, my network regularly shares job opportunities with me that they think I might be interested in, based on the conventional expectation that I should be in a job role inside an organization. It's nice to be considered, of course, but the fact is I'm not looking for a new job role. Knowing that I don't have to fit into anybody's idea of convention except mine is truly liberating, allowing me to express my viewpoints opposing discrimination more freely and with greater ease, unconstrained by an organization's politics. There is a real freedom in this which enables me to pivot in my work as I need to.

At the start of my consultancy career, I had a number of meetings with board directors and senior leaders of the major UK sports organizations, presenting what I saw to be some of the industry's biggest challenges when it comes to issues of race and ethnicity. I was met with nod-heading platitudes of acknowledgement and agreement with a promise of follow-up. Years later I'd still be waiting for that follow-up. This was a common occurrence for me at the time, and I realized that it didn't matter about my experience, my master's degree in education, my longstanding nationally recognized and award-winning campaigning and antiracism work; the fact was that these kinds of organizations just weren't interested enough; the best I received was some responses citing a lack of funding or other, more pressing priorities than tackling equality issues. Yet, if these organizations faced up to their lack of ethnic and gender diversity, this would support their ability to meet their other business objectives. The rationale is clear, especially given that we know from McKinsey research that there's a 35 per cent dividend business payback – a payback that's intellectual and in part financial – for companies that have a representative workforce when it comes to ethnicity and gender.

I also knew that my uncompromising and unapologetic way of articulating the facts of racial inequities in sports wasn't a comfy and cosy chat and that this therefore didn't make me palatable to industry leaders. Their pretended empathy and interest were frustrating. Organisational psychologist John Amaechi OBE often refers to this pretence and feigned empathy as being more dangerous than forms of open contempt when it comes to redressing racial inequities in organizational systems. This is something I and many others working to redress inequities have experienced and can certainly relate to.

I quickly realized I wouldn't be able to make money from this avenue of work and redefined my career journey again, as is often the way for Black people. For me as a Black woman, asking white people in power to commission my services and undertake racial equality work sat uncomfortably and still does, if truth be told. I decided to back myself and identified new ways to create financial income. If you let it, oppression can rob you of your dignity, and on this occasion I used my own capacity for self-determination to render that oppression powerless to control my opportunities.

Both these scenarios serve to illustrate the ways in which we can regain power in our lives by creating a new lane and a new box with your own terms and conditions. I exist outside the conformist, conventional box of being a CEO.

Tools of resistance

Navigating the fine line of 'choosing your racism battles' from one day to the next while having to exist both inside and outside organizational norms and conventions is the Black experience. Black people's occupation of internal spaces can only ever be temporary and conditional and so they must simultaneously exist outside such spaces if they are to survive being on the inside. This is often the only space where they can truly achieve and excel.

We are all leaders who have the ability to redefine our lives and organizations. There will undoubtedly be mountains to overcome but with the right mindset and techniques we can all create our own real wins for success. Breaking down stereotypes and codes of privilege is more layered and complex for some compared to others. The common thread is that we can each increase our self-awareness and take responsibility for our lives by defining our versions of success and work towards that.

There is power in understanding yourself within the inherently discriminatory systems you find yourself in, but there is more power in how you reimagine yourself *outside* these systems in the hope for a better future. In the next chapter we will explore how you take responsibility for your life by standing in the power of your most vulnerable truths.

Real wins

- Checking the evidence of past achievements and tuning into the power of your identity and heritage can help break the confidence deadlock in moments of stress.

- It is the responsibility of organizational leadership to unlock the access codes of privilege and develop structural interventions that create antiracism outcomes.

- The better we understand ourselves, the greater clarity we have to define and design success on our own terms.

- Define what success looks like for you and hold yourself accountable to this rather than an organization's limited vision of your success.

- See how operating outside gendered and racialized expectations will lead to greater rewards personally and professionally.

- Black people exist outside the boundaries of convention and conformity in all of their layers because there's no other choice if we really want to achieve our truest and highest potential.

4

Standing tall

Drawing on the strength of my heritage to sustain me
to take the risks, to go all in, despite the fear.
Taking the time to heal, to lament, to go again,
Self-love means speaking and standing in your truths
regardless of how uncomfortable it makes others feel.
Michelle Moore, 'Declaration of Independence'

My head snapped up as I felt the hair on the back of my neck prickle and my temperature start to rise. I looked into the face of the man in front of me – I'll call him Kevin – his face neutral. I chose my words and pronounced them with deliberate calmness: 'Can you repeat that? I didn't quite catch what you said.' (This is the tried-and-tested technique I use whenever I hear racism; sometimes, when the person hears their words back, they think twice and try to backtrack at speed.) My words landed, echoing through the drab room where we were gathered for our meeting. I was the only Black person in the room of ten people. I'm not going to repeat the words that were said to me because so often when Black people recount stories of racism they are met with ambivalence and denial. In this instance Kevin's words confirmed age-old tired racist tropes and stereotypes that are not even worthy of the ink of this page.

I was in a meeting working with a media organization where I was presenting proposals to radically overhaul the HR recruitment procedures to diversify the workforce and increase their ethnic diversity. I could tell Kevin had picked up on my stiff body language and I sensed his impatience, but chose to ignore it. He was on a roll. He continued in an exasperated tone: 'Don't go all PC on me, Michelle—' I stopped him mid-sentence before he could say anything more. 'Kevin' – I paused to make sure I had his attention – 'what you've just said here is highly offensive.' Kevin held an important role in the organization and had a lot of influence, so I made a quick judgement call that perhaps the best way to deal with this would have been after the meeting, away from the eyes of the junior colleagues also present.

Kevin was taken aback by my response. I could see in his face that he realized what he had said and whom he had said it to – perhaps when he looked at me on that day, he didn't see me as a Black woman; he saw my lighter skin tone and believed he could get away with spewing racist tropes. He started to look uncomfortable and yet his egotistical nature wouldn't let me, as the manager with the least status in the room, call the shots. He shifted uncomfortably in his seat and started to disagree, but I had already stood up, looking him dead in the eye with a hard, uncompromising stare that dared him to continue. He stopped talking, the room was silenced except for his quickened breaths, the others watching intently, the air stilled. I gathered my papers and left. At the time I regretted not giving an immediate, well-articulated Afua Hirsch-style clapback. There was something about that moment that was different; it was as though I had been robbed of my words, I was so profoundly disappointed. I was tired of all of it all: walking the tightrope, playing the game, even as I strived to stand in my values. Something snapped within me that day.

The system had won; it had beaten me down. In truth, it wasn't even that one event; it was a lifetime of rejection, sly subtle digs, negative racial assumptions, lower pay, the code switching ... you name it. That's what oppression does: it creeps around your edges, slaps you firmly in the face and then unforgivingly repeats the cycle.

I knew the procedures for reporting such incidents, but I also knew the potential ramifications. To my surprise, I had no fear. It was like everything had been leading up to that moment somehow, and this was an instant where I could play big or play small. I calculated the risks and decided zero action wouldn't equal any change. I reported it to Human Resources. As with any institutional politics, it became a long and protracted affair as Kevin initially denied his words with a dogged determination, then eventually accepted he had used those words and gave what he thought was an apology (you know the kind where someone says, 'I apologize if I hurt your feelings'). I wasn't interested in a half-assed pathetic non-apology, though. I wanted Kevin to be held accountable in the same way that other employees would be: a formal warning, a suspension or even a removal from his position.

My actual boss seemed to have deserted me and wasn't interested in supporting something that felt controversial to him, making it clear to me that he didn't entirely believe what he kept referring to as 'my version of events'. On top of that every time I walked into the office, I could feel the eyes of my colleagues on me, judging me while not talking to me about it; one person went so far as to tell me to drop it because I was causing too much tension in the office. My already heightened state of emotions and my colleagues' responses made me start to doubt my own understanding of what had happened. I felt like I was under water, drowning in my own anxiety while everyone else stood on the water's edge pretending not to see me as I went under. I had been ostracized. It was a lonely place to be. Division and exclusion were the order of the day. Their refusal to hear my accounts and their allegiance to the status quo left me stunned and wounded – a wound so palpable I actually felt the sharp edges of the blade on my skin.

It was a stressful time. My night terrors had returned, though I wasn't sleeping much, as I kept replaying what had happened inside my head. The emotions triggered other experiences of exclusion. This is what racism does to you. It impacts your mental health and results in you questioning your own mind. It increased the release of the cortisone stress hormone into my bloodstream, and I felt as though I was on constant high alert, my emotions dancing on pins. My family was worried about me. *I* was worried about me; my fearlessness had deserted me. But, as so often when you are at your lowest, you are given a glimmer of hope. I was offered a lifeline in the form of an executive coach – Lou, a kind and astute Black woman. In our first meeting her words sustained and rejuvenated me. 'It's true, Michelle; it happened in the way you remember. You're not going mad, and you're right in what you're doing.' It felt like that first gulp of oxygen you take on breaking the surface after holding your breath under water. I wasn't losing it, my mind hadn't been playing interpretation tricks on me, it was all true. It was a transformative moment, and as if a switch had been flicked I let go of all the negativity and toxicity in a moment. Lou's belief gave me strength. My sanity was restored. It was all level, and I was back to deuce point.

As there often is in these kinds of situations, there was a loophole that Kevin could escape through. I had to accept that, despite the ruckus and real reckoning the organization was being forced into, Kevin would retain his position and face no repercussions. This wasn't a surprise to me. The experience had taken from me but I wasn't done despite the injustice of the system. I decided to fix the loophole. My sister was flummoxed as to why I would choose to do this for an organization that had treated me so badly. I was convinced that I didn't want this to happen to another person from a marginalized identity who might think they had no power. So, I produced new diversity recruitment guidance for the organization with clear sanctions. It's often the way that it's the victims of racism who become the very people who use their skills and talents to rectify parts of the broken system.

Tools for leaders

Creating policy that is sustaining, accountable and robust is fraught with challenges and needs concerted efforts from the collective. It's not the responsibility of one lone individual to fight for justice or of the victim to become the saviour.

I understood the system and how to navigate it, yet, despite this and having right on my side, it appeared like I had still lost. Black people are always having to make the sacrifices for the greater good. This reminds me of when I interviewed the three-time WNBA Champion basketball player Renee Montgomery, who in June 2020 had been the first professional athlete to sit out of the 2020 basketball season and sacrifice her playing career to fight for social justice and against systemic oppression as part of the Black Lives Matter movement. When I asked her about *her* sacrifice for the greater good, she responded: 'It has been like this from the beginning of time. This is not something we are not used to.' Sport is full of athlete activists like Renee who tirelessly use their platforms to call out racial injustices, and my own small example of challenging racism in the workplace is in part inspired by the likes of Renee and her WNBA compatriots. Renee uses her power and individual agency to make a stand, building on the legacy of historic sports activists from the days of Tommie Smith, John Carlos, Wilma Rudolph, Kareem Abdul-Jabbar and Muhammad Ali.

The very last meeting I had with the senior leaders of the organization and my boss is etched into my memory. The meeting took place in a basement meeting room, where the walls were dressed in dull grey blankness and there were no windows. I remember thinking it was OK because I felt light. The lack of comfort offered by the mercilessly hard chairs and the height of the table meant that I couldn't sit properly, my knees jammed against the underside of the table. Such was the importance of this meeting that not only my boss but also his boss and his boss were seated before me. A bevy of bosses. One of them was verbally drawing a line underneath the whole situation. I appeared to be listening, but in truth his voice was like the very low background noise of a TV programme you're not that interested in but keep watching anyway. I looked at them with sadness and pity in their privilege and whiteness. They were still regurgitating the organizational equal opportunities policy rhetoric, knowing all the same that they had failed to uphold it at every single point of the process. A part of me was tussling with the fact that they were not bad people, just cogs in a bad system with none of the tools or, more importantly, without the courage to even attempt to dismantle a small part of the organizational racism of which they were a part. They were just as oppressed as I was; they just didn't know it. To them I represented a controversy that they wanted to disappear. In my eyes I had won; yes, Kevin was still in his position, but the organization had been rocked. So, as I looked into their eyes, an inner confidence and calmness descended upon me. I could feel the legacy of my ancestors; in those moments of triumph and loss I never feel alone. Yes, I was battle weary, but I was brimming with my own power and ancestorial pride. I'd accepted the outcome while fiercely and morally rejecting the system and the complicit parts my colleagues had played in it.

As the boss finished talking, they waited for my response, I paused and decided to respond with action: I stood up, asserting every inch of my six-foot-one frame, looked them all in the eye, paused and saw their slight squirms; that's what happens when people know they are in the wrong but still try to front that they are not. I no longer felt caged by the circumstances and refused to be their prisoner for one second longer than I needed to. I was standing in my power; I gave an almost imperceptible disappointed shake of my head and walked out of the room for the final time, while inwardly notching up one of my most painful 'real wins'.

This is a common story that many from a marginalized identity can relate to: calling out the injustice, followed by denial from the perpetuator, gaslit by peers while pushing for accountability and trying to manage the subsequent mental health effects. Racist tropes can seem like the smallest of incivilities to some white people, but this is because of the sophisticated way in which racism plays out in everyday language where it can easily be denied. Black people, however, know and feel when racism rears its ugly head. The unravelling of my particular situation revealed how deeply the structural layers of racism had become entrenched within the organizational culture. My power didn't result in Kevin losing his position, but, in calling out the racism and the policy creation, I'd forced the organization to face their racism. I used my personal power in lots of different ways to achieve this. Finding your power and sense of agency is the key to transforming your experience and ultimate liberation and finding your own real win in these instances. Although seasoned in experiences of discrimination, I had no idea this would become such a protracted and toxic process with all kinds of political and conflicted interests muddled up with racism and privilege. I wish I could have been forearmed. Later in this chapter I'll be offering you your very own resilience kitbag.

The people or the organization?

I often hear organizational leaders, especially those working in sport, say that when racism and discrimination are gone from society then organizations won't have a problem anymore. John Barnes, a former professional footballer for England from the 1980s, is famous for saying that racism is not football's problem but society's ill. It's always frustrated me why this is such a popular statement; given the cultural capital of sport, surely it should be leading the way? Why do we have to wait for society to change first? Surely, sport can and should play its part, be proactive? I don't think this is an ambitious ask.

The fact is, organizations are made up of people who make up society, and people spend a lot of their time in organizations, so it stands to reason that we have to tackle the issue at an organizational level. Both systems and processes need to be in place to ensure that there are consequences to overt and covert forms of discrimination and incidents like the one I've described. Often, an organization can have all the policies and procedures in place and yet when confronted with the issue it fails to enforce them. This is especially the case when it comes to race. The real fear of being called a racist has white people running to the hills. If organizations followed their own procedures in the same way they do with any other complaints, issues could be resolved more efficiently.

To be antiracist, white people have to refrain from centring their own whiteness and accept that they have to seek to understand the experiences of Black people. This has to be done without making Black people responsible for their own education. I've worked closely with white leaders inside organizations and on boards who say they are committed to tackling racism, and yet there have been a number of occasions when they have outright not believed me when I have raised an issue of racism, be that stereotypical marketing campaigns or outright racist statements.

On one such occasion I was giving the leaders of a large charity feedback regarding the lack of ethnic diversity on a national judging panel; the leaders did not accept my insights and chose not to follow my counsel. Six months later, after having read an article by a white academic who writes about white fragility, the leaders took on board my insights and to their credit recognized their defensiveness, apologized to me and redressed this in their company policies. When Black people raise issues about discrimination they must be believed. White people must recognize that they have no lived experience of Blackness. They must rise above their defensiveness and acknowledge that Black people have the knowledge and expertise they do not have. This is absolutely not to say that white people can't have empathy, but no amount of empathy or proximity to Blackness will provide white people with the lived experience of being Black. Having Black friends, a Black partner or Black children does not enable you to experience having a Black identity. This is a wider truth that needs to be accepted not only by white people challenging racism for Black people but also, for example, by straight and cis-gendered people standing up and advocating for members of the LGBTQ+ community and non-disabled people campaigning for disabled people's rights. When we stand for and with each other, our rejection of inequalities and our shared empathy are strengthened.

Tools for leaders

White people in positions of senior leadership must accept their privilege and understand that it is incumbent upon them as members of the dominant group benefiting from oppression to tackle and dismantle it. Social justice and greater equity for everyone happens only when we all stand for each other, because in the end we are all interdependent.

Standing in your power

Being able to develop and sustain your professional and personal resilience when you experience racism or discrimination requires certain tools of self-care. You may find yourself in situations where you think 'I shoulda, woulda, coulda' and spend inordinate amounts of time after an incident wishing you had responded differently. I talk candidly to the people I help about how it's not the responsibility of the person being oppressed to always challenge the oppression because of the emotional tax you're already carrying in the world if you belong to a marginalized group. This particularly speaks to the emotional tax and labour Black women suffer – the additional barriers they face, their unremunerated efforts, and the harms they experience, and the harmful and toxic impact all this has on their mental health. In her talk for *The New York Times* events, the US activist Brittany Packnett writes powerfully on how Black women's unique oppression in the workplace is revealed not simply in lost wages, but in 'lost time, in lost energy, in energy wasted', even if, despite this 'emotional and cognitive tax', Black women thrive. '[W]e just shouldn't have to,' she finally declares.

Tools of resistance

Standing in your power in those moments is deciding how you're going to respond or not respond while maintaining perspective, understanding that your act of resistance is protecting your emotional health and wellbeing.

If you decide to challenge an incident, either at the time or retrospectively, the key is to feel as empowered as possible in your approach. By being forearmed, we can label the negative emotion when it arises and have the armour to cope with the impact of it. When in these situations I ask myself three questions:

1 Is it worth it? (How valuable is this relationship to me?)

2 What are the personal consequences to me? (How will this affect my career and my mental health?)

3 What is the bigger question? (How does this fit into my strategic life plan? Is there another time or another way I can challenge this?).

These questions can be used to fit your individual context and can help you to reclaim your power and find your own Serena Williams-style 'game, set and match' comeback statements.

The UK author, broadcaster and professor Gary Younge describes racism as a system of control. Where the least dominant group has no control, it is up to you to employ the techniques of what you can control while remaining true to yourself and prioritizing your wellbeing. The impact of discrimination unfairly gifts Black people thousands of daily opportunities to build up moments of fearlessness by strengthening their muscles of courage. Being courageous is not always about the fight; it can also be about embracing all aspects of your identity. When you see yourself more clearly in your own identity, others see that too, and in turn they see more of themselves.

Tools of resistance

For the victims of racism, the acceptance and rejection of injustice is twofold. Understanding how the structural system of racism works is in fact rooted in our resilience and ultimate survival. Knowing this information actually helps you to label it, see it coming, better understand it and comprehend the bigger picture.

It has taken me a long time to stand in the power of my own identity and truly own it. At times I have assimilated underneath the white gaze because it didn't feel safe enough to speak my truths. It was easier for me to as a lighter-skinned Black woman of mixed heritage to avoid conflict, fit in and climb the career ladder. The toxicity of colourism decrees that the lighter your skin tone the more desirable and the less intimidating you seem and as a consequence you are less likely to be a victim of racism. My experiences are therefore minute compared to darker-skinned Black women and the daily threat of racism and intersectional oppression they face.

As your personal growth expands alongside your political consciousness, you may find – as I did in the opening story here – that you are prepared to challenge the status quo in new ways. Through my actions, white people were confronted with their own privileges and the complicit roles they played in the systemic racist structures of an institution. They were called to face up to their own biases as part of their identity, which is why it was such an uncomfortable experience for them. If you're from a minoritized group, you have no choice and are used to discomfort, though you shouldn't have to be. This is where resilience enters the arena.

Resilience

Resilience can be hard earned, but when it's in your possession it becomes priceless. Having resilience can provide you with endless supplies of energy – and we all need that to reach for our goals (I know I needed it in bucket loads to help me become more accepting of my friend Perri – perimenopause!)

Psychologists define resilience as the process of adapting well in the face of adversity, trauma, tragedy, threats or significant sources of stress – such as family and relationship problems, serious health problems, or workplace and financial stressors. According to the American Psychological Association this is achieved 'through mental, emotional, and behavioural flexibility and adjustment to external and internal demands'. Crucially, in a 2013 article Angie Hart and her colleagues optimistically offer that resilience is 'overcoming adversity, while also potentially changing, or even dramatically transforming, (aspects of) that adversity'. Being resilient is an important element of success. It is critical in enabling Black people and marginalized groups to not just survive, but to find ways to thrive in their professional environments.

I think of resilience as a kitbag of equipment that you pull out when you need it for competition time. The bag needs to be regularly replenished with kit so that you never run out of anything. If you don't have enough kit, your performance will be impacted as it is impossible to give more than you have. If you ever try to, it will likely have negative consequences on your mental and physical health. Resilience doesn't discriminate; we all need it because we all face adversity in all areas of our lives, whether it's the death of a loved one, a divorce, an illness or bankruptcy.

One sunny June morning my resilience was tested on two fronts. My nerves were stretched, my brow furrowed and my throat tight; my whole body felt constricted. A close friend had suddenly passed away. The circumstances had been traumatic – it was heart-breaking. I went into work a few days later to collect some things so I could work from home. I looked and felt terrible; desolation felt like a cloak upon my shoulders. I'd worn this grief cloak before and knew how it felt to be dressed in its misery. I didn't want to see anyone but of course I did; a colleague approached me, took me by my arms and said, 'I'm sorry. I didn't know ...' I remember looking through her and not quite at her in my dazed state of grief, thinking that she was going to pass on her condolences, but instead she continued in a shocked tone: 'I didn't know that you're Black.' She peered at me as if I was under a microscope. My immediate reaction was a kind of half-laugh, half-cough. I was in disbelief that this colleague could be so tactless and unaware of the impact of what she was saying. It was so odd and so completely unexpected, even if, as soon as it was said, I wasn't surprised in the slightest.

This may seem like an almost trivial story to share, and perhaps you might think this colleague of mine was purely innocent in expressing her shock, but the outcome was far from that for me. A part of me found it very strange given how I fully embrace my identity as a Black British woman, especially within the work environment. What my colleague was signalling to me through her ignorance was that, whether she realized it or not, she hadn't acknowledged my Blackness as my identity and that she wasn't going to hold it against me now that she knew this information. This is part of the misunderstanding of mixed-heritage identity. In her essay 'The Meghan Markle Effect', the UK journalist Phoebe Parke explains that, if your physical appearance is more European, then 'we're assumed to be white until further notice'. I think this is what my colleague had assumed of me. This instance tested my resolve and resilience. I was spent emotionally and physically exhausted from grief, and, to top it off, I was having to deal with this nonsense. Race and resilience are the two never-ending strands of an intertwined rope. The extraordinary US writer and activist Audre Lorde expressed this brilliantly when she said that being Black in a white space is a political act in itself because of how White supremacy creates a hostile environment for our very existence. During those fleeting moments in the office that day, I certainly felt as though I had been thrown into a lion's den.

Your relationship with resilience is a personal one and dictated by your intrinsic motivators, preferences and the things that make you feel more like yourself. However, there are some basic principles that underpin resilience. When we master our mindset and accept that adversity is part of the life cycle that affects all of us, and we focus on what you can control, this helps us to keep negativity in check. 'Benefit finding' psychology is another bedrock of resilience – in other words, finding things to be grateful for even in the midst of utter anguish. In a TEDxChristchurch talk that has been viewed over a million times, researcher Lucy Hone asserts that simply asking yourself 'Is this helping or hurting me?' can help you to bounce back from some of your biggest challenges; by asking yourself this question each and every time you find yourself in a moment of despair, you can recover from adversity and personal tragedy. It's a question that puts you back in the driving seat of your car, giving you control over your decisions. These kind of approaches are by no means a panacea and they don't remove all the pain, but they have been scientifically proven to help you process what is happening, to recognize that recovery is possible and that there's still hope. In moments of grief and challenge, above anything else we need hope. I'm reminded of the words of the legendary motivational speaker Les Brown when he *said,* 'If you fall, fall on your back. If you can look up, you can get up.'

'You have to become spiritually ribbed,' the writer and broadcaster Afua Hirsch preached. These are not her words; she borrowed them. In 2018 I was at a book event with Afua and the well-respected historian David Olusoga. Afua had arrived late because she had been at a special event where billionaire media executive and philanthropist Oprah Winfrey had been present as she was in the UK promoting a film. Afua had asked Oprah about what Black people needed to survive in an environment not set up to benefit us. Oprah had responded by telling her that anyone who is facing some kind of oppression must be as 'spiritually ribbed' as possible. This lesson stayed with me, and I believe Oprah was referring to the resilience that comes out of self-care.

There are many different ways to stand in your power, but this has to be built on a bedrock of resilience – just like when I was an athlete: I knew that there were daily things that I could do as part of my everyday life outside of my training that would help me become better, more resilient. Taking responsibility for your life is about how you stand in your power in tough moments, by embracing your strength and vulnerability at the same time. This is built on resilience. Developing a resilient mindset and consciousness as an ongoing lifelong habit during the times when you are *not* experiencing adversity means that, when the bad times do show up, your kitbag is full and you have the strength to cope.

Below are just a few tools that I have used to ensure my kitbag is full. There are, of course, many other tools, but I've found the following ones the most useful. I'm sharing them with you so that, when the unexpected happens, you have your spikes, your track vest, and, above all, that resilient mindset.

Confide in your support crew	Share your life journey – the highs and the lows – with a group of people whom you trust and who champion you.
	Acknowledge and honour your feelings and share them with a friend, especially if you are experiencing any form of oppression. Sharing with others who have experienced oppression means that there is an automatic shared empathy and compassion. The smallest gesture from a friend can make a big difference to your current and future resilience levels.
	Engage with people who make you feel seen and ask for their help. This shows that you value yourself highly and that you understand that your vulnerability isn't weakness.

(Continued)

Use positivity tools	Listen to your favourite podcasts, rest and undertake daily affirmations.
	Spend time with friends who make you laugh or watch comedy shows.
	Make time for laughter, dance, meditation and play, and find moments for joy whatever that looks like for you.
	Celebrate yourself and your identity. This is part of creating a strategic joyful resistance for any people who feel oppressed. The Black Joy movement in the summer of 2020, at the height of the Black Lives Matter movement, was a key counter to Black pain.
	Keep a journal – e.g. morning pages – to get everything out of your head onto the page; it's miraculous what can emerge and the guidance this can give you in your daily decision making.
	Get a daily hit of Vitamin D. Even if it's raining, get outside!
	Get active, whether that's taking a daily walk or competing for a sports team.
Practise gratitude	Complete a daily gratitude diary of the five things for which you are most grateful. Even if you don't get to write them down, think about them. Research has shown this to be a powerful method for achieving greater fulfilment in life, helping you to appreciate your life.
	For 30 days reach out to people by email or text to tell them how they have positively impacted your work and life. I did this mainly with work colleagues and acquaintances and it proved a powerful exercise to show my appreciation for the support and lessons I have learned from others.

Be of service	Be of service to others – this has worked for me when I've been at my lowest. It leaves you with a sense of profound satisfaction that you can be of service to someone else and helps to release your focus from your own challenges and regain some perspective. Kindness translates into resilience power.
'Know thyself'	Invest and work on your personal growth and get to know your patterns. For example, when I have delivered something that has gone well and I'm on a high. I know that once it's over I can often experience a very low mood, so in order to get over this slump I plan an enjoyable activity for the day after a big event or talk.
	Celebrate your big and small wins by rewarding yourself with whatever makes you happy. It's understanding that the small moments add up to the big moments in life that creates the real wins, so acknowledging your achievements is paramount.

Tools of resistance

Self-care is a component part of resilience as it helps sustain you and create the elasticity of hope and possibility that we need to create your 'real wins'.

The depths of my own despair

I was hunched over my kitchen table, head in hands, drained and rung out. I looked again at the figures on the laptop screen at my bank account balance and realized that the colossal mistake had cost me thousands of pounds. I'd made a foolish decision due to severe fatigue. I'd been averaging two to four hours of sleep a night for what felt like months. It felt as though there was a huge rock in my throat, and my chest was tight with anxiety. My sense of powerlessness and dejection was almost overwhelming. Everything had built up to this moment: it was not only the financial loss, it was the sense of helplessness that I couldn't find a way out from this place where I was so weighed down with anxiety and sleeplessness. I distinctly remember the moment because it's the first time in my life when I thought that this is what it must feel like to be suicidal. I was in a dark, dark place.

I was navigating the early throes of menopause. My body was suffering from extreme hormone deficiencies, causing me emotional and physical distress – severe brain fog, anxiety, sleep disturbances, irregular periods, severe joint pain, memory loss, hot flushes ... There are 32 symptoms of the menopause, and I've named only a few of mine here. I was 43, which was too young, I first thought, to be going through this, though I soon had to admit it was the age my mum had entered the menopause. Genes rule, so it was my time, too. I was in the perimenopause – the time during which your body makes the natural transition to menopause, marking the end of your reproductive years.

I fell victim to the 'strong woman' trope, thinking I could handle it when, in reality, I couldn't. I was unwittingly also playing into the 'strong Black woman trope', which absolutely did not serve me. For Black women, the experience of the menopause is surrounded by silence and stigma. Historical patriarchy and racialized tropes based on shame about sharing our natural experiences as well as the stereotype about not showing weakness are big factors impacting Black women's experience of the menopause. This further reinforces the stereotype that Black women are strong, which results in medical racism: research has shown that medical professionals believe that Black women can withstand higher pain thresholds than their white counterparts.

As in society more generally, in the West Black women are on the margins of discussions about the menopause. There is a small yet mighty cry from Black women menopause networks for greater representation in the imagery of how menopause is portrayed and a call for more research into menopause specifically in relation to Black and Asian women because race and cultural background are neglected in current studies and the education of General Practitioners (GPs). Menopause power and awareness are on the rise. With over half of the workforce made up of women, organizational leaders need to be aware of the impact the menopause has on women and their performance in the workplace, and especially of how Black women experience menopause symptoms differently and more adversely than white women. We need the world of sport to also wake up to the impact of hormone changes on athletes' performance. Olympian Jessica Ennis-Hill has been leading the way with this, specifically looking at hormones and menstruation. With leading experts in women's hormonal health, Jessica has created Jennis

CycleMapping, an app that empowers women to truly understand their bodies and hormones, showing them how to train, eat and sleep for optimized hormonal health.

Sometimes life slaps us in the face and forces us to slow down. The perimenopause did this to me, and to some extent it is still doing its work. I saw myself as emotionally and physically resilient, but the perimenopause had other ideas. That low moment was a turning point in my menopause journey where I knew I had to get help fast. I accessed hormone replacement therapies and got my life back. It wasn't an easy journey to access the support and specialist knowledge I needed, but I did it by drawing on my sports mindset of accepting the current reality and problem solving at each different barrier I experienced. I had to be the best advocate for myself even when I didn't have the mental strength to be so, drawing on all of my resilience reserves.

My daily rituals – meditation, celery juicing, gratitude practising, daily walks, journal writing – became essential in managing my emotional health and wellbeing, so I increased them. I used my mindset to make friends with my perimenopause journey and accept that my new friend – aptly named Perri – is here only for a short time in my life's journey. I can't say I've come to embrace her but I'm now more at ease with her. Perri is teaching me to be kinder to myself, both mentally and physically.

Self-care tools can undoubtedly have an incredibly positive impact on building resilient leaders. However, there is a health warning that goes with this, especially for people from marginalized groups. Some of the trappings of resilience are that an individual can be perceived as strong and not in need of help; even when they show their vulnerabilities they are not entirely believed. Black women have to be strong in the same way other individuals from other marginalized groups have to be strong if they are to face and overcome the oppression they experience. This imposes an additional and unjust burden where resilience has helped to develop this strong sense of self-efficacy – a burden that itself can be a cause of trauma. If we think about this in the professional context, Black employees are expected to take on the additional tasks of antiracism work on top of their normal roles; this was especially the case in the wake of the racist murder of George Floyd in May 2020. Many Black people were burdened with increased, unremunerated responsibilities and expectations around leading the education of their organizations in responding to the Black Lives Matter movement.

There are pitfalls to resilience that have to be carefully considered, however. One is what I call the resilience self-efficacy trap, of which a key dimension is the 'Be strong!' trope. In 2017, a close friend passed away from breast cancer; she was a beautiful human being and still is a beautiful spirit whom I carry in my heart. We spoke openly and candidly about her terminal prognosis in the weeks and months leading up to her passing. She became very sick and would often complain to me how much she hated the many texts she received telling her to 'Be strong!', which held no solace for her, living as she was with a terminal prognosis. Now, I know that this is an extreme example, but it's a lesson that has stayed with me, because there are so many other ways to support people when they are in the midst of a crisis – from offering to just listen to sometimes crying with them. The next time I'm ever tempted to say or forward that 'Be strong!' text/meme, I'll think twice about what would really support someone's resilience mindset.

This chapter has shown you that standing in your power is about when you're ready to take emboldened actions in life for yourself and on behalf of and in service to others. This shows up for each of us in all kinds of ways. This agency when channelled can create an energy and fire that can be transformative for you and your communities. The key is to recognize that the many different routes to personal growth are rooted in identity and a commitment to do the inner work of resilience which gives you power to tackle life's challenges in ways you couldn't have imagined for yourself. We have looked at some very specific practical tools to help you stand fully and majestically in your power; the next chapter will examine the losing and winning mindset in leadership.

Real wins

- Organizational leaders must level up, accept and receive feedback from Black people and acknowledge the injustice of racism by ensuring policies are not merely created but meaningfully enacted.

- Reclaim your power by taking personal responsibility for your life, allowing yourself to feel fear and yet stand in your power.

- Our success is rooted in our common humanity: when only some of us are free from oppression, none of us are free from oppression.

- Become 'spiritually ribbed' by committing to the inner work of building your personal and professional resilience.

5

The opportunity in leadership

I think of it as one of the moments of reckoning in my career. It happened one grey afternoon when I was a new manager; I was the youngest, the boss and the only Black woman in my team. A member of my team approached me and said that the team needed to talk to me about my management and suggested I listen not to respond but to understand; it was invaluable advice that I didn't quite appreciate at the time. We had a meeting where the team laid it on the line about my leadership and management style and what they felt was my overbearing, demanding and autocratic approach. It was a tough listen. I didn't respond, I literally couldn't. I was shell-shocked. When I'd started as their manager, I did what I thought was good leadership work: I shone a light into all the dark corners and bought much needed clarity and structure to organizational processes and accordingly received praise from my bosses. I'd read dozens of leadership books and took them to heart, leaning on the US leadership writer and leader Max De Pree's words 'The first responsibility of the leader is to define reality'. It's within this context that my team's feedback felt bewildering because we were getting results and I thought that they understood that, underneath my stern façade and forensic examination of their work, I respected and held each and every one of them in high regard. It felt like a first-round knockdown sucker punch in the solar plexus, as if I had been unceremoniously knocked flat out on my back, landing with a loud thud onto the cold, hard and unforgiving ring floor.

Immediately after they left my office, I was in so much distress that I called my dad, who told me to carry on and to go back into the main office like nothing had happened and face them out. I agreed and promptly did the opposite; my dad generally gives stellar advice but, on this occasion, he slipped up. I had to honour my feelings. I had to listen to my emotions. I needed to be alone to process what I'd been confronted with. I left the office, sobbed during my car journey home, and then reset myself that evening (which involved crying it through with a friend). The next day I went in like Anthony Joshua in his comeback fight victory over Andy Ruiz Junior. I was used to winning and getting back up again from my athletics days, and I knew how to make my own comeback – to square my shoulders and resolutely and resiliently hold my head high as I faced up to the situation. My team's feedback felt unfair, but deep down I intuitively knew that there were fragments of truth in their words, that aspects of my no-nonsense, micromanagement style would have to be adjusted and some of the language I used softened.

It was a bitter pill to swallow which I still feel in my throat years later.

That day I thanked my team for their feedback and acknowledged that, as much as it was a hard listen for me, it must also have been awkward for them to articulate their truths. I laid out the changes I would make and asked for their support and understanding as I worked through that. The team member who'd initially approached me stayed behind and told me how impressed and proud she was of how I'd handled the whole situation. 'Is she patronizing me?' I thought.

Even as I thanked her, I wrestled with my internal suspicions of a hidden, racialized subtext. Experience had shown me that, when you exist in a space that's not built for difference, there's always a subtext to everything; hidden dynamics of power and race are always at play, whether it's understood or not. I was guardedly wise to sophisticated forms of racialized undertones, especially in some of the loaded language choices regarding my perceived 'aggression' which played into the 'angry Black woman' trope. My six-foot-plus frame (I've lost count of the times I've been called overbearing for standing still), my direct approach and race affect how people relate to me, but when the racism is covert you can never be entirely sure it's at play. Discrimination heightens sensitivities to such an extent at times that your expectations of racism can at times be unfounded, albeit, in my experience, this is the exception to the rule.

I had to accept that the positive self-perception I held of my leadership and management style was not held by my team. I believe that my leadership style was largely based on my high-performance sporting mindset. As an athlete you receive constant feedback from your coach so that you keep refining your technique so as to execute a winning performance. This meant that I was used to working within my own mental framework of performance and marginal gains thinking. Although this mindset has continued to serve me well in my career, on that occasion it didn't because of the very particular work dynamics at play. My sporting mindset had helped to create unrealistically high standards for myself and others. At that time, I lacked the emotional intelligence to understand the different ways you can inspire and get the most from teams within a professional context. I had to listen to better understand and with more awareness than I ever had before; I had to be vulnerable, to self-reflect and make changes to my leadership style. It was a huge personal challenge, and I had to wrestle with a lot of internal conflict.

I adapted my 'autocratic' style by creating systems which increased collaboration and team autonomy. I did this by implementing new ways of working that focused on sharing leadership responsibilities. One simple example was increasing time for more strategic conversations about the outcomes of senior management meetings and organizing for team members to present proposals at those meetings rather than me. I spent more time developing and nurturing relationships, getting to know the individual strengths of my team and playing to those strengths. If I'm really honest, I found developing some of these relationships tricky. I knew to get the best out of the individuals on my team I had to develop genuine trusting relationships. I created greater transparency across the team, so everyone was aware of responsibilities and workload. As hard as it was, I understood that for at least one member of my team I was never going to be the person who got the best out of them. I therefore organized for that individual to receive external mentoring, and he undertook some work shadowing of another senior manager. It was an unravelling and painful leadership journey for me, yet I soon realized that, in creating this greater shared responsibility, I also created greater collective ownership of the vision and work. Although it was testing, surprisingly it ultimately served to support me, and I felt less lonely in my leadership role.

It took some time for me to regain their trust, but my changes gained respect and eventually approval from my team. It certainly wasn't a 'happy ever after' scenario, and certainly no smooth execution of the perfect 400m hurdles race; it was more like a succession of stuttering moments over the course where the stride pattern goes a bit wrong. Nonetheless, all in all, for the time I was their manager, I managed to execute mostly trouble-free vic-tories. I suffered from the very common 'I want everyone to like me' syndrome, and in truth not everyone in my team did, but what they did do – which was evident in their behaviour towards me – was respect me. I had to accept that being a vulnerable leader in those moments also created the pathway for excellence, as the team went on to achieve far greater results in performance and productivity. This 'career reckoning moment', although obviously not one of my most shining moments, was in its own way a real win because I turned it around and took on board the tough lessons and made changes to my leadership style. I learned that leaders have to accept their fragilities and embrace all aspects of their identity.

As the Swiss psychiatrist Carl Jung described in his 'shadow' concept of the self, we are each made up of both lightness and darkness. The darkness describes those aspects of the personality that we choose to reject and repress. It is this collection of the repressed aspects of our identity that we don't like that Jung referred to as our shadow. When other people draw our attention to aspects of our shadow, it can cause a lot of distress and a deep sense of injustice, so we can be tempted to push those parts deeper into our unconscious psyche rather than facing them. When my overbearing and demanding management style brought my shadow into the light, I had to learn to embrace it, which created the space to move from defensiveness and denial to compassionate self-acceptance of myself and my truths. A conscious leader is prepared to do this self-awareness work, so they show up as authentic, grounded and well-rounded individuals accepting all of the contradictory elements of their own identity.

In this chapter I will explore why leadership is important, what it is in its purest form, and the now urgent need for socially conscious leadership. I will highlight that we all have the innate skills of leadership and can make a real difference by owning that opportunity, whether you're leading yourself, your family, work colleagues or the community.

The case for conscious leadership

I'm often asked about leadership as though it's some mysterious and exclusive undisclosed secret sauce only available for a short time to a limited number of people. The truth is that we are all leaders because we are leaders of ourselves. In its simplest form, leadership is about the conscious choices we make when we care about something enough, and, crucially, *conscious* leadership focuses on the present moment and our current state.

The beauty about conscious leadership is that it gives you the opportunity to define it for yourself. Theoretically at least, conscious leadership is where an individual is committed to learning, deeply curious about themselves and others, and therefore has high levels of relational connection to them. Conscious leaders are able to access high levels of emotional intelligence and are innovative in their approaches to work, believing that learning and growing are more important than being right. By contrast, leaders who lack the skills of conscious leadership operate from a space of blame, judgement, ego and entitlement and view winning as their most important determinant of success.

Our world is increasingly divided socially, politically and environmentally, a division that favours the wealthy and underserves the most vulnerable. A new wave of conscious leadership is urgently needed. As I write this, the world is in the midst of the COVID-19 pandemic and still wrestling with the ramifications of the brutal racial murder of the African American George Floyd in May 2020. If there's ever a time for an uprising of conscious leadership, then that time is now. The leadership of movements can be conscious, too, based on more collaborative group-centred models of leadership rather than traditional, often hypermasculine ones, best demonstrated in the three founders of the most influential protest movement in decades, Black Lives Matter: Alicia Garza, Patrisse Khan-Cullors and Opal Tometi. The fundamental elements of conscious leadership are based on authenticity, integrity, empathy and accountability. Conscious leaders listen with the intent to understand and not just to respond, and they do it by being in tune with themselves and the world around them.

Leading the individual

The number-one determining factor which enables a child to learn is the enhancement of their identity, and it's the same for adults in many ways, too. Part of being a conscious leader requires seeing and valuing the identities of all the individuals in your team.

We are often led to believe that leaders of sports teams will be the strongest athletes, highly skilled in communication, and with an ability to inspire and motivate others. Yes, of course all of these qualities contribute to great leadership, and it's quite clear that these qualities make a big difference in team sports. However, we rarely hear about what can sometimes be perceived as the 'softer' skills of being the captain, those of empathy, belonging and identity. The sense of belonging and enhanced identity that the captain brings to a team as a part of their leadership skillset is, I believe, the difference between good and excellent leadership. This really struck me when I interviewed former England netball captain Ama Agbeze whose leadership approach involved her motivating, rewarding and valuing each team member and giving them the confidence to recognize their unique contribution and their part in creating a winning culture:

> As the captain I felt I should understand what motivated each individual and show them how much I appreciated and valued their contribution to the team. I bought gifts to make them feel special before our matches. The gifts represented what it is to be English. Initially, I gave everyone a rose and bought small gifts from the Body Shop, Cadbury's and other well know shops of English origin. I made videos which featured each player and talked about what binds us together. At the Commonwealth Games I gave them family photo frames painted with the England flag.

I was a bit surprised and impressed by the level of detail and the lengths Ama went to to find different gifts for every player, demonstrating how in tune she was with their individual personalities. The level of respect that comes from that kind of genuine care enhances the team's shared identity and purpose. These symbolic gifts created a greater relational trust which translated into individual and team success. Ama is a naturally empathetic individual who was always prepared to do what she asked of her team and who understood their personal and collective challenges. In 2018, Ama went on to create history in captaining the England team to a dramatic Commonwealth Gold victory.

Kate Richardson-Walsh OBE was the captain of the England hockey team for 13 years and the most capped female hockey player in England history. She led the national squad to Olympic bronze in 2012 at the London Olympics and gold at the Rio Olympic Games in 2016, and in so doing becoming one of the most famous hockey stars in English history. Over the years Kate built a strong team ethos and commitment to win that drove the team to Olympic, European and Commonwealth Games success. This was not always the case, as she shared with me in our conversation. Initially, Kate struggled to adopt the mindset and behaviours to lead the team. Being young and inexperienced she found it challenging to manage her own performance on the pitch, let alone the performance and motivation of her teammates. In 2004 as a young 23-year-old captain the team failed to qualify for the Athens Olympic Games. It was a tough spot for Kate as she had to re-evaluate her leadership style and cope with the huge disappointment she felt not only for herself but the other players, the large majority of whom were on the brink of retirement, their Olympic dreams dashed.

This ignited a fire in Kate for the rest of her career, and she channelled that defeat into a new leadership path. Kate understood that her leadership had to be more than what is typically viewed as a part of captaincy – leading on the pitch, putting on the armband, saying the right words in the huddle, and setting a good example – because this type of leadership was limited and didn't bag the global medals. Through a period of learning and deep self-awareness Kate developed her leadership style by owning her vulnerabilities and learning through her mistakes:

> I had to listen to their truths. There were times where I felt I was genuinely helping the player by saying certain things in a certain way and they'd feed back to me – when you say this to me this is how it negatively affects me, which obviously hurts like hell to hear, but it's a lot harder for them. It's about being open to that. You have to put your defence mechanism down and take it in and actually listen to them and their truth because that is how you're making them feel, regardless of how I meant it and it came across, and some of that feedback was massive for me.

In being open to their honest critique of her leadership and in the sharing of her fragilities with the team, Kate deepened her own understanding of leadership and was able to create a greater sense of belonging, trust and relatability. Over the years, and perhaps unknowingly, Kate has been playing into elements of conscious leadership, and along the way Olympic gold became the happy by-product.

I wanted to know what Kate – now retired from hockey – has learned from sport that she now uses in her corporate role:

> Taking the temperature in the room is something I learned as the captain, to take an honest view, not

what I think or what some of the biggest voices are telling me. Getting a sense of where the energy is at and where it needs to be. Being in tune with each other, how we sense energy, how we read each other (or over-read, as you can make the wrong judgements). So, it's the feeling, asking and not prejudging something that I've learned the most.

By honing her talents of active listening and 'taking the temperature' in the changing room on the hockey fields, Kate was able to understand the individual needs of her teammates and what they each needed to give their best performance. This has now translated into her corporate career to great effect.

'Leader-ful' feedback

In the early 2000s I was working as a Community Manager in a large inner-city London secondary school. The headteacher, Anne Barton, had a charismatic, quiet yet strong way about her. During a one-to-one meeting Anne had given me some feedback about my work, telling me that I was doing a good job and had unique talents nobody else in the school had. I waited patiently with bated breath to see what else she was going to say in her deliberate, quiet, slow way. Anne told me that I that I related well to the young people, parents, teachers, governors, Local Authority folk, the youth workers at the local community centre, funders and role models I insisted on bringing into the school. She broke it down for me, explaining that my gift was to use my influence for the benefit of others, especially when introducing new roles models into the school and advocating for the children and their families. Above all, she said, I drew out the potential in others. I was somewhat underwhelmed as I felt like this was everyday stuff that most people could do. My days on the track had taught me to be open to feedback and to take my coach's words seriously. It's a skill of leadership to receive feedback well, and sport had prepared me well to receive this input from Anne. But even though I didn't quite realize it at the time, in that moment Anne had gifted me a valuable leadership lesson.

What was powerful in that moment is that she saw me ... I mean *really* saw me. She saw my talents and my unseen labour that I thought nobody else saw and she praised this in a way that made me understand more fully their impact. Anne was role-modelling conscious leadership here because, when she praised me, it was both in private and public and even when I wasn't in the room. Later on in my career this became something I always tried to do as a part of my own leadership style when managing teams. Anne saw my potential when I didn't see it for myself and gave recognition for my unseen contribution. In that moment she taught me that, even though I had limited management experience, I had the capacity to flex my leadership skills through the power of my influence, identity and authenticity. Whatever level you find yourselves in an organization, from entry to middle to senior level, or if you're an entrepreneur, you display and live into your leadership potential through using your influencing power as part of your leadership skillset.

If Anne Barton had told me to jump off a cliff I would have done. Why? The school was 'requiring improvement' when I joined, and the senior leaders were systematically and determinedly turning it around. It felt as though we were all in it together, in much the same way netball captain Ama Agbeze and hockey captain Kate Richardson-Wash instilled feelings of unity and teamwork where everyone felt as though they belonged to something bigger than themselves. For me, this created the sense that, even though I had limited management responsibilities at that time, I felt like a leader and that we were all leaders signed up to the same cause and working to the same vision. African American political activist, academic and role model of mine Angela Davis wraps up this point perfectly when she argues that, when done right, leadership is a *collective* experience: organizations should have multiple leaders, should become 'leader-ful' as opposed to leaderless.

Nurturing and developing the talent of those around you in small and big ways to become leader-ful is one of the bedrocks of outstanding leadership. Being truly seen by those around you – which, disappointingly often, may not include your managers – is immensely powerful, as I showed in Chapter 2 where we explored visibility. Enabling team members to become leader-ful and filled up with new knowledge, skills and understanding creates valuable moments, experiences and opportunities for professional and personal growth. Within the context of conscious leadership, people perform better when they are supported. If each one of us decides to become a reflective leader regardless of our status within our organizations, we choose to do the work of self-reflection, investing time in understanding and learning how to achieve in our own areas of development.

If you are leading others – whether you're leading a team of one or one hundred – conscious leadership is more than identifying a course to improve a perceived weakness of an individual. It's about getting underneath limiting beliefs, curating and creating space for learning, and deep strategic conversations which move people on and out of their comfort zones. It's encouraging team members to attend external high-level meetings with people outside of their normal peer group. It's ensuring that one-to-one management meetings address personal development, and it's about reward and recognition at both the public and private level – from work shadowing and mentoring to secondment opportunities and on-the-job training and development. Conscious leaders think creatively, knowing and understanding their team members and what can make the difference for individuals' personal growth while inspiring them to reach for their own personal best and 'real win' moments.

Why leaders may need to give up power

Athletes are good problem solvers. The more experienced I became as a manager, the more of a trouble-shooter I became. I was known for getting things done and resolving problems. On one occasion I needed to get to know a new team and area of work quickly. It was early January, and I was chairing my first meeting with my new team. 'I don't think you quite understand the nature of this work,' Joan informed me. An awkward silence followed as the rest of the team waited for my response. I was a bit taken aback, as Joan couldn't quite hide her condescending tone; it just crept into her voice as she finished her sentence. Because she was very experienced in this subject area, I couldn't help but feel a bit intimidated. However, at that stage of my career I'd been around the leadership and management block a few times and learned the value of deep listening and owning my leadership vulnerabilities. 'I agree, you're right,' I responded. Instantly, the atmosphere in the room changed as the team sat up and waited curiously and intently for my next words. I made a quick decision and told them that I would work-shadow them in their roles and then do their jobs once I'd learned the ropes. I still remember their sceptical faces looking back at me. It was unheard of for a senior executive to be undertaking tasks that would have deemed not compatible with my position. I'd decided to 'walk my talk' by taking on the role of my new team of junior staff who were operating at a project administrative level. 'Walking the talk' in business is where actions are aligned with values. One of the most effective ways to do this is to lead by example, and this can often mean giving up some of your power as a leader.

It was an invaluable experience: for two weeks I learned more about the role and challenges for my team than I could ever have imagined. I also gained the respect of my team, earning valuable social capital. The experience enabled me to accurately represent their needs to my senior manager, reward their work and make the necessary changes which benefited the team and the wider communities we were serving.

Tools for leaders

All good leadership starts and ends with effective self-leadership.

A part of being an effective and reflective leader is letting go of having to know it all and have all the answers and trusting in your team, something I was working hard to address as it didn't sit well with my high-performing mentality. By taking on this junior role I'd actually put myself in my very own stretch zone where my ego was professionally challenged, but I knew that, in order to be authentic and at the same time get results, I had to do this. A conscious leader is prepared to give up their perceived power and stand in their truth, all while owning their vulnerabilities. Because of this, they are able to stand in someone else's shoes, acknowledging, and able to empathize with, their truths.

Giving up power and enabling others to play their leader-ful part has been my ethos as a leader throughout my management career. At times, this has been born out of necessity. Despite being an effective manager in nurturing talent and innovation, I often wonder how much more successful and effective a leader I could have been if I were white; if I hadn't had to deal with the feeling that I was living a half-life, not ever fully living into all of my potential. The institutionalized racism that is seen and unseen coupled with sexism and ageism impacted the success of some of my leadership responsibilities and meant that I knew was on the losing side (somewhere, as you've probably gathered by now, I don't like to be). As a by-product, this would have had an adverse impact on the growth and development of the different teams I've worked with throughout my career.

As unjust as this was, I became wise to it and learned to navigate it in order to protect my teams. As a conscious leader with a commitment to the desired outcome, at times I chose to move over, both literally and figuratively, and share my leadership responsibilities when I knew that a white member of my team would likely be received more favourably. If I was white, I might have got further in my career, but I probably wouldn't have been a better equipped leader. Because I am Black and because of the hurdles I've had to overcome, I'm a better leader. Perhaps that's the unfair reality for many Black leaders.

Leading diverse teams

Conscious leaders understand that leadership is a collective experience, and to create a winning team the team has to include a representation of people from different backgrounds, whether that pertains to race, gender, culture, sexuality, disability, socio-economic status, religion or age. All this is well rehearsed and easily understood by many, but in truth the enactment of diversity poses an epic challenge. Hence the shoutout here: we can't talk about leadership without stating the obvious because leadership without diverse representation is poor leadership.

Recognizing this greater diversity will introduce healthy cognitive dissonance to homogeneous teams, which is what all teams need to create high productivity and creativity. This kind of leadership isn't rooted in the age-old 'We tolerate all people' nonsensical rhetoric (a pet hate of mine – as if I want to be 'tolerated') but arises out of a deep respect and reverence for understanding difference and all that it gifts.

Tools for leaders

Seeing and valuing the backgrounds and identity of individuals in your team, and understanding the enrichment this brings to strengthen all aspects of the team and the work, is a part of conscious leadership.

Everyone knows that appreciating and respecting difference is an integral part of managing diversity, but it's often not truly comprehended and meaningfully actioned. To do this, senior and middle managers and leaders must understand the nuances and the overlapping ways in which discrimination interrelates based on an individual's identity *in all its aspects*. As Audre Lorde – writer, feminist, womanist and civil rights activist – highlights, none of us is just one thing and leads a single-issue life. One of the main issues is that leading and managing teams of people from a wide range of backgrounds requires managers and leaders to be skilled enough to manage and understand the different perspectives and styles of learning and communication, and to harness this to achieve the team goals. That is why, as I mentioned in Chapter 2, high-quality leadership and development training are required to ensure an organizational workforce fit for purpose. Practice has to be intentional and thought through, taking into account the different leadership styles required of you within the boarder context of leading teams with greater diversity. The UK sports industry suffers from the lack of diverse representation across the entire workforce, particularly at senior and middle leadership levels.

Tools for leaders

The greater the organizational representation, the greater and quicker the solution-finding happens and the more successful the team.

Leadership and management of the UK sports industry

I want to apply some of the conscious leadership concepts I've just outlined to reimagining the leadership of sport in the UK. By doing this, I will highlight why the leadership and governance of sport in the UK could do with a healthy dose of conscious leadership (albeit these general underlying principles can be applied globally to the organization of sports). If the leaders of sport decided to do the self-awareness work of self-leadership to accept their white privilege, to listen so as to understand the negative experiences of Black communities, to move over, give up or even share some of their power and status, the UK sporting landscape could look very different from what it does today. Let's first briefly set the scene.

On the face of it, Great Britain is a successful sporting nation. However, you don't have to look very far to see the stark inequities that exist for people from Black communities, for marginalized groups and those from low socio-economic backgrounds. The structures and organization of sport in the UK are overwhelmingly white, male and middle class. It is the most monocultural industry in the UK.

Research has revealed the racism, sexism and bias that poisons the very roots of the UK sports ecosystem, covering everything from the teaching of physical education in schools to elite performance sport, from media coverage to representation on boards and in coaching positions. Muslim women are the most marginalized of all groups, having very little access to sport due to limited pathways and islamophobia and the intersectional oppression they experience. The whole sports landscape needs a radical overhaul. At the height of the Black Lives Matters movement of 2020, Chris Grant, board member of Sport England and one of the most senior Black administrators in British sport, called for a South African–style truth and reconciliation commission to tackle structural racism in sport: 'the inequalities are so deeply rooted within sport's structures and assumptions that the situation amounts to a kind of apartheid hiding in plain sight'. For decades, he pointed out, UK leaders of sport have been seemingly apathetic and therefore resistant to addressing racial inequities in sport. In June 2020, this lethargy was disrupted by the tragic and racist killing of the African American George Floyd at the hands of the US police force.

From the sports activism of UK Black athletes who powerfully articulated their experiences of racism on the front pages of the press, to the phrase 'Black Lives Matter' replacing Premier League players' names on the back of their shirts, to players 'taking the knee' at the beginning of games, racism has become the talking point in UK sport. Black athletes in the UK are using their voices in new ways to highlight endemic racism and the disproportionate impact of COVID-19 on their communities. As the Black Lives Matters movement gathered momentum and worldwide media coverage increased, and given the huge social and cultural capital sport holds, sports bodies were left with no option but to respond. Sports organizations rolled out press statement after press statement denouncing racism and promising to do better. It is an indictment in itself that it took the tragic murder of George Floyd to galvanize the UK sports industry into starting to tackle racial inequality.

Sport should and could be leading the way in fighting racial inequality; that it's not is because there are serious failings in its leadership and governance. Leaders in the industry frequently articulate what they think they want or perceive the solutions to be, but these are invariably not what sport actually needs, resulting in knee-jerk diversity and inclusion interventions that never get to the root cause of discrimination. Leaders often want a dot-to-dot approach without understanding that to systematically redress racial inequities they also at the same time need to challenge their own biases and racism, which can be a challenging journey of self-discovery. Imagine if leaders took responsibility for these personal and collective failings and held themselves accountable for their own learning and any gaps in their understanding while also deactivating their 'fragility receptors' – getting over the immediate defensiveness and denial response (rooted in white privilege) and accepting that racism is entrenched in sport. Redressing racial inequality in sport needs leaders to step up by increasing their own levels of self-awareness and take on the self-reflective work of conscious leadership, because this lends itself to antiracism. Antiracism work is in part a personal learning voyage that in turn positively impacts the collective organization and whole sports ecosystem. Another dimension is for those in leadership to get to grips with creating cultures where people take radical responsibilities to commit to seeing everything as an opportunity to learn and grow.

In this way, accountability and responsibility could become the cornerstones of a new conscious style of leadership and could provide the foundations for redressing racial inequities. This process requires sports leaders to take out the parts of the system where people can make bad decisions by setting up effective rules, policies and legislation. Lack of access, opportunity and representation in leadership positions is the serious fault line in UK sport. As an example, despite the fact that the media often stereotypes Black people as being naturally sporty, Sport England research shows Black children are less likely than their white counterparts to meet official guidelines for the amount of time spent in physical activity each day. Black sporting success might be visually conspicuous, but the barriers to Black people leading a healthy physically active life is sadly hidden. Structural racism limits talent pathways and access to facilities, funds and specialist equipment, among many other things.

Conscious leadership not only comes with great responsibility but also a self-awareness of personal and collective vulnerabilities. When you understand that creating equity for the most marginalized in any society benefits everyone in that society, it becomes a real win for everyone. The leaders who are prepared to be part of meaningful action have to do the work of accepting their own individual and organizational shame and become resilient to it and then consciously do something about it. Being this kind of conscious leader means that you're aware and personally responsible for the impact you and your teams have on the world – in this case the impact racism has on Black communities in sport.

The personal responsibility aspect of conscious leadership extends itself to the question of power in sport – who holds it and how they use it is *the* question. For example, the leaders of sport must reckon with the impact of intersectional oppression on Black women because they account for just 1.2 per cent of positions on the boards of 39 sports organizations, as revealed by a *Telegraph* sport investigation. In June 2020, Dame Heather Rabbatts, the Football Association's first female board member and the first ever Black board member, revealed that gender targets in sport have mainly benefited white women.

The levelling up of individual, organizational and collective responsibilities in the sector is what will create a sea change. Mistakes will be made, but my hope is that, as we discussed in Chapter 4, these mistakes become the lessons learned. Leaders must be consciously intentional in all areas of addressing racism. Author and lawyer Dr Shola Mos-Shogbamimu extends this point in a CNN interview when talking about the complete lack of diversity at the 2020 BAFTAs (the UK equivalent of the Oscars). She asserts that it is the undermining pervasive nature of indifference translated into action that feeds the toxicity of inequality both consciously and intentionally among those in positions of power to bring about change.

This work is as much a personal journey of transformation and healing as it is a collective race of reinvention and overhaul. The leaders of sport need to be part of a movement of change where they accept the complicit roles they play in upholding the racist status quo and embark on the conscious leadership work of dismantling a system of oppression. There is no short cut to strategic thought-out antiracism work – in doing the unravelling of your own inherent racism you develop the consciousness to apply it to your context – and when you start to get to grips with the deep learning that takes place, you're then empowered to recognize the actions needed in your areas of expertise.

An overhaul of the sports landscape involves developing antiracism approaches and frameworks rooted in ongoing conscious leadership training and development delivered in creative ways. This might be truth and reconciliation roundtables, reverse mentoring or performance-related pay linked to antiracism targets. There is, I believe, a need for an urgent and forensic examination of every part of the sports ecosystem – an ecosystem that is broken in terms of not only governance but also investment, legislation and participation – and subsequently a mass mobilization of the sector to create change within a new system. This kind of radical rethink would serve to create a seismic cultural shift that moves far beyond the jazzy slogans, performative actions, and falsehoods of organizational vision statements. Change is urgently needed to create the conscious leader mindset and cultural shifts to create a fairer sports landscape for all. This approach also requires leaders to have clarity about their values.

Aligning your leadership values and purpose

Effective leaders know themselves well; they understand their strengths and have a clear idea of their values and what they stand for. These strengths and values can inform tough decisions in times of crisis. By identifying what you truly care about, you can better navigate challenges and make choices that reflect those values. Defining your core values can help you make tough decisions and keep you grounded in your integrity. This clarity can make life easier, especially when your values are not upheld by the wider organization or culture, whether that's in a work meeting or in communication with a friend. In my career I've been in environments that have refused to validate and acknowledge my contribution because I've stood firm in holding and articulating my values. It was a lonely experience, but my values became my anchor and I held on to them as tightly as I could as they felt like the only true things I had going for me. I wasn't going to wait for permission to lead, and it was my values that provided me with the inner strength to understand this. I learned that I had to lead from the very position I was in, regardless of my then current status or lack of authority as perceived by others. Leadership can take place upwards, sideways and in all kinds of ways. I used my values as if they were my own superpowers and walked my talk. When you live out your values, you're demonstrating the best kind of authentic and conscious leadership for yourself and others.

Athletes often describe getting into the zone – that elusive state of flow where performance is effortless and where all the elements of technique, environment and motivation come together to create a personal-best winning performance. I've only experienced this twice on the track, and the only way I can describe it is as being similar to what I can imagine an experience of transcendence to be: I felt as if I was effortlessly running on air, unfeeling of my body and environment, as if I had entered into another dimension of consciousness. Something similar occurs when leaders are congruent in their beliefs, values and purpose and the work flows with ease and doesn't feel like work. This alignment creates the environment to operate from a space where you are in a state of flow and you are your most authentic self. Alignment is not necessarily about excellence or being first; you're not obsessed with your competition but striving for a deeper confluence of what's important to you and your teams, connecting all of you to something bigger, more rewarding and often of real social value. True alignment results in 'real wins' for an individual and for the team. If you can tap into those moments of alignment based on your values, this creates the space for more conscious leadership of yourself and others. Let's reimagine a world where the leaders of sport can take this on by living out values of justice and equity to redress racial inequality. This approach requires action and activism in all forms. This is what we will discover in Chapter 6.

Real wins

- We all have the ability to be conscious leaders by accepting our fragilities and embracing all aspects of our identity.

- Giving up the power of titles, status and positions leads to ultimate liberation for the individual and the collective.

- To be the leader of any group of people we have to be prepared to create an egalitarian ecosystem of distributed leadership where everyone is enabled to play their 'leader-ful' part.

- The leaders of sport must tackle systemic racism and intersectional oppression by taking individual and organizational responsibility and implementing antiracism principles.

Identity and activism

I had rehearsed and rehearsed. I knew my script word for word, yet I was still nervous and excited: I was about to come face to face with one of my all-time heroes and role models. I had met him before, but this time it was different. It was going to be my honour to interview African American former sprinter Tommie Smith as part of the 2017 Runnymede Trust annual lecture being held at the University of Manchester. As part of my role as a Runnymede trustee I had been asked to interview Tommie after the lecture to the 800-strong audience as part of this special occasion celebrating the fiftieth anniversary of the iconic salute at the 1968 Mexico Olympic Games. Tommie Smith, alongside his teammate John Carlos, had become household names in 1968, a year full of global unrest and social change. They were two of the fastest men in the world and became legendary names in sport after they proudly raised their black-gloved fists on the medal podium, having won gold and bronze medals respectively in the 200m. Their raised fists have remained symbols of resistance, hope and activism ever since that transformative moment.

So, you can understand my excitement over interviewing such a courageous and inspirational figure. I poked my head around the door of the auditorium. It was packed full of people, and there was a buzz of anticipation in the room and I felt myself becoming even more exhilarated. I walked to the green room to say hello to Tommie and his wife, Delores. Tommie remembered me from two years ago when I'd met him for dinner during the London 2012 Olympic Games, and we greeted each other warmly in remembrance of that occasion. We had a brief conversation about the format of the interview, and I did what I always do with this kind of interview, reassuring Tommie that my job was to merely shape the conversation and to make him feel as comfortable as possible to speak his truths. 'Let's go, folks,' Omar, the director for the Runnymede Trust, called out and motioned for us to make our way to the auditorium.

We walked into the packed auditorium to roaring applause – it was a special moment. My first job was to introduce Tommie. Steeling myself, I walked to the lectern at the front of the stage and started to give my introduction. I spoke from the heart, sharing how nervous I was, and even though my voice was shaky I told the audience what a great honour it was to sit beside and talk with one of the world's greatest athlete activists. I deviated from my script, as I often do, by coming out from behind the lectern to show the audience my special

T-shirt which had the Tommie Smith salute printed on it. I proudly showed it off and shared how I'd had the iconic image on my wall since the age of 16, the salute forever etched in my memory as a reminder to use my personal agency and power for the greater good. I raised my voice and spoke with a certainty and clarity in that self-assured way you do when you're inspired, moved and just plain grateful: 'Throughout Tommie's life he has suffered, sacrificed, endured and ultimately triumphed. His tale is of a strong Black man who overcame the forces that were crushing him – yet he is still on fire with a smile on his face. We are honoured to have him with us. We are in the presence of greatness. Give a warm Manchester welcome to Tommie Smith!' There was rapturous applause as I welcomed Tommie onto the stage. He greeted me kindly with a big hug and a mouthed 'Well done!' I could tell he was touched by my words and how grateful I was to be in that moment with him – he could sense it. I drew comfort and strength from his embrace. I was in the right place at the right time, everything in alignment and as it should be; this was a truly exceptional, almost spiritual moment for me. I felt light. I felt alive.

The interview was a powerful and deep conversation filled with light and dark moments where Tommie recounted some of the devastating impacts the iconic salute had had on him and his family, including death threats, exclusion, stigma, media vitriol and the International Olympic Committee lifetime ban on his participating in the Olympic Games. Tommie explained that both he and John had stood proudly on the podium wearing black socks in lieu of shoes to depict the poverty Black people faced in the USA and that the salute was made in solidarity with the American Civil Rights struggle as a part of the Olympic Project for Human Rights. One of the most powerful lessons he imparted was about the power of redemptive sacrifice, which he explained as something that is only open to us when we understand who we truly are. He asserted that self-awareness is at the heart of all activism; that challenging any kind of oppression is about truly understanding yourself and the potential impact of your actions, while deeply knowing what it is that enables us to take action or to not take action. The audience, myself included, were spellbound by his words, in awe of his humility, courage, wisdom and humour. There was something very emotive and evocative about the atmosphere that night; it was literally fizzing. The audience felt the weight of history and Tommie's majestic spirit and energy.

At the end of the interview there was a long and rousing standing ovation. So many people can identify with Tommie's story, be inspired by it and at the same time educated by it. Smith's story resonates because, worldwide, Black people and those from marginalized identities are rooted in the same struggles. In the wake of our rich conversation I was brimming with emotion and thankful that I had honoured the commitment I had made, to myself and others, that I would enable Tommie to speak as freely and openly as possible. I had succeeded, and it felt good. Tommie gave me a heartfelt hug of gratitude, as did his wife Delores; both had enjoyed the interview. It was a lifetime memory, and one of my favourite and definitive 'real wins'. At the end of the event, I was part of a small group who went out to break bread and have a meal back at the hotel with the Smiths. It was a magical evening and an amazing way to end a very special night I'll never forget. Smith gifted me a signed poster, which is now framed and takes pride of place on my living room wall. I felt so lucky and still do, forever grateful to have had the privilege of interviewing one of my all-time heroes.

In 2012 I had been fortunate enough to meet the other half of this activist duo, John Carlos. I had attended one of his talks when he was in the UK. John gave a stirring address about his experiences of that time, and I was literally sitting on the edge of the plush red cinema seats. The venue was the Ritzy Picturehouse in Brixton, which has been a cultural home for many Black Londoners for decades and an apt venue for John's talk. I asked him what was going through his head as he stood on the podium. John said that he remembers wise words of advice from a conversation he had had with Dr Martin Luther King, who told him that the Mexico Olympic Games represented a huge stone thrown into the ocean, creating ripples that could change the world, and that John and Tommie's act of protest had stood up for those who couldn't stand up for themselves. His words resonated deeply with me, reminding me about being of service to others, and how in such acts of service we can unwittingly create change that can be far-reaching in its impact.

The courageous actions of John and Tommie created one of the most enduring and iconic sporting images of the twentieth century, resonating across the globe. Their sacrifice was immense, their inspired action luminous, as they stood up for their beliefs, full knowing the price they would pay. We can all relate to Tommie and John's story on some level because, whether we realize it or not, at some point in our life we have all been in a minority of one or two and know what it is like to stand up, even if it's just in your office or at a family event, and articulate a different perspective. Perhaps their actions can inspire you to make your own stand-out moments of activism in small and big ways in your professional and personal lives as you make your authentic contribution to the causes you are passionate about. I celebrate and am emboldened by Tommie and John's legacy, though for you it might be Billie Jean King or Muhammad Ali.

Many of our freedoms today are a result of protest. American author Dave Zirin explains the iconic moment of the salute as providing the perfect marriage of 'Movement and Moment', enabling it to become a statement for the ages. Historical moments like this provide the legacy for contemporary sports activism. Fifty-four years later symbolic acts of protest in sport are still seen as hugely threatening. The International Olympic Committee banned athlete protests at the 2020 Tokyo Summer Olympic Games, and in the wake of British football fans booing professional footballers for taking the knee in support of racial justice at the start of games, senior members of the British government described the actions as 'gesture politics'. It's an age-old trope used to silence and veto all forms of protest. It's vexing, but also revealing. The symbolic power of protest through sport is a potent combination in our society and shows why actions such as the Black power salute or taking the knee are so impactful and troubling to authority. Perhaps this was best summed up by comedian and *The Daily Show* host Trevor Noah in a 2020 monologue, at the height of the global Black Lives Matter movement, when he said: 'There is no right way to protest because that's what protest is. It can't be considered "right" by the system its protesting.'

The role of an activist

Many of us, at some point in our career or personal lives, have to stand up for something we feel strongly about, just like Tommie and John (albeit probably not to the same degree). This may come in many different forms, but the chances are that, as you seek to redefine your goals and resist stereotypes, you will be both activist and sometimes, by default, unwilling enforcer. In the last five years, sport has seen a new wave of activism from the likes of Colin Kaepernick, Serena Williams, Raheem Sterling, Simone Biles, Megan Rapinoe, Ibtihaj Muhammad, Naomi Osaka, Lewis Hamilton, Caster Semenya, Maya Moore, Kadeena Cox, Bilqis Abdul-Qaadir, LeBron James, Alysia Montano, Cori 'Coco' Gauff, Allyson Felix, Nadia Nadeem, Ada Hegerberg, Eniola Aluko ... The list goes on and on. These athletes have been galvanized by some of the biggest social and political challenges of our times, from gender, racial and LGBTQ+ equality, to intersectional discrimination, unequal pay, body image, working conditions, abuse and basic human rights. These phenomenal athletes have used their platforms to shine a light on social injustices. Sport is intractably linked with politics and therefore is a powerful form of protest because of how it engages with the mainstream and can puncture the views of those in privileged positions unaffected by systemic oppression. As the US writer Dave Zirin says, 'Sometimes an athlete has to say it before people can hear it.'

Most people don't necessarily see themselves as activists, but I believe it is open to all of us who care about injustice. The power of activism can create movements that lead to societal and global change, whether that's decades or days in the making. I like the term 'activism' because it is powerful. I choose to view 'activism' within the context of justice, individual responsibility and social change. Interestingly, the word 'activism' is becoming increasingly popular in the circles I work in, although not so long ago it was almost a dirty one. I was once advised by a well-intentioned colleague not to use the word in a pitch I was about to present to a corporate audience, because for them it would conjure up the idea of 'trouble' and she suspected I, too, would be viewed as a bit of a troublemaker. I didn't take her advice on board, being acutely accustomed to the white gaze and white policing of my work. Unsurprisingly, my pitch was unsuccessful.

Funnily enough, in some ways I agree with my colleague – I *am* a troublemaker – but there's good trouble and bad trouble. As African American Civil Rights titan John Lewis, in his 2014 commencement speech at Emory University in Atlanta, said: 'You must find a way to get in trouble, good trouble, necessary trouble.' This reaffirms another lesson I learned from the John Carlos's talk in Brixton. John spoke about the negative publicity he had received after the salute and one particular headline stood out for him – 'JOHN CARLOS TROUBLEMAKER' – leading him to recollect all the true greats who had also been called troublemakers, from Malcolm X to Rosa Parks. He decided he was in good company.

My rationale henceforth was clear: any potential corporate clients who didn't like me using the word 'activism' weren't the right clients for me. This was me being authentic and standing in my values. I find it interesting when it is assumed that to create change you somehow have to fit into the existing structures, even though those structures were not created to benefit Black people or marginalized identities. So, to excel and progress within the system, the expectation is that the individual bends, flexes and assimilates, or, in this small example, uses the words that a business deems acceptable. Perhaps earlier in my career I would have towed the line, but by that point I was confident enough in my activist role and what I could contribute to choose to walk away from the pitch and use my campaigning skills to lobby for change outside the organization. From experience I believe organizations benefit from both internal and external activism in redressing racial inequality. Roll on two more years and the company realized it wanted good trouble and invited me back.

Tools for leaders

Change in organizations happens through people internally and externally taking on activist-like roles. Activists on the inside of organizations use their understanding of the institutional politics and marry this with expertise gained from the activism of those external to the organization.

The small axe

As the world has become increasingly divided, social change activists have been at the heart of the struggle for social justice. Sport has seen new levels of activism, and the word 'activist' has become more acceptable and fashionable. I see activism taking many forms in the campaign for equality. It might be stepping up in your own life to resist any form of prejudiced or racist views, asking your teenage son to stop using the word 'gay' as an insult, calling out an uncle who strongly asserts his racist views about immigration at a family gathering, or challenging a work colleague complaining about all the media coverage Kamala Harris received as the first Black woman US vice president. I want us to view activism in its broadest sense of 'creating social change'. Writing this book could be seen as one form of activism. Throughout this book I'm challenging you to think differently and to perhaps consider new ways of being in the world. For me the type of activism I advocate is about challenging views that are steeped in racism, sexism, misogyny, homophobia, xenophobia, ablism and classism; to be an activist is to be someone who wants to redress these forms of oppression.

I believe that sport can lead the way because of its assets of cultural and social capital, and that athletes themselves can be catalysts for social change. If activism is life affirming, then athlete activism can inspire us to pursue our own form of social action, however small we perceive that activism to be. Everyday actions of activism are unromantic, tedious and monotonous but nonetheless build up pressure and can help forge new coalitions to create individual and collective social change. This is best summed up by the African proverb 'If you are the big tree, we are the small axe', meaning that even the mighty can be brought down by small and sustained action. In November 2020, BAFTA and Golden-Globe–winning filmmaker Steve McQueen created the highly anticipated *Small Axe* anthology of films, each focused on telling a different story of the West Indian community in London. One of the films, *Mangrove*, is based on the actual trial of nine Black activists falsely accused of inciting violence at a protest demonstration in 1970. The 'Mangrove Nine' were acquitted after a 55-day trial at the Old Bailey, England's Central Criminal Court, alongside the first judicial acknowledgement that there was 'evidence of racial hatred' in the Metropolitan Police.

The 'small axe' African proverb was popularized by Bob Marley in his 1973 song of the same name. Marley's lyrics are about people power, unity against tyranny and a trust in the greater good. The song focuses on an evil figure (the big tree) who exploits inequality for power and reasons of vanity. Bob represents the people (the small axe) as being wise to the pretence of the evil figure, who is not as clever as he looks and can be 'easily broken' in the struggle for the greater good.

Mangrove makes powerful, if disturbing, viewing. I was moved by it and reminded about the many historical lessons of activism. We have been here before, and there is much wisdom and inspiration we can draw on. I reflected back on those courageous nine individuals, especially the titan writer and racial justice activist Darcus Howe and activist Barbara Beese, who were members of the British Black Panthers and who courageously chose to self-represent themselves in the biggest court in the UK. It's fitting that Steve McQueen chose the title *Small Axe* for his series of films, in which the activists are perceived as the 'small axes' compared to the 'big tree' of the Metropolitan Police and its legal team.

The story of the Mangrove Nine stands alongside another landmark milestone in the fight against racism in the UK, the brave and resolute struggle of Doreen and Neville Lawrence against the Metropolitan Police as, for more than 20 years, they pursued justice for their murdered son, Stephen Lawrence, who was killed in a racist attack in South London. The sacrifices of the Lawrence family in their fight for racial justice and equality are immense, with Doreen eventually taking her battle for justice and equality to the House of Lords as Baroness Lawrence of Clarendon, the power of her particular axe now gigantic. Our debt to the Lawrence family can never be repaid. I am reminded about my very 'small axe' contribution to sport and social activism when I worked for Charlton Athletic Race Equality (CARE) Partnership in the 1990s, an organization set up in direct response to the racist killings of the young Black men Rolan Adams, Rohit Duggal and Stephen Lawrence.

Tommie Smith and John Carlos, Barbara Beese and Doreen Lawrence, can all be viewed as individuals with a 'small axe', but it's still an axe that can deliver blows with a mighty, concentrated force. But wielding that axe can be painful. There is no comfortable way to bring about change especially when fighting for equality.

Where can you apply the 'small axe' philosophy in your life? Wherever and however you find your 'small axe' to create the change you want to see in the world, don't be discouraged by its size but let yourself be empowered by its power to defeat even the biggest and fiercest opponents. If equality and the greater good are on your side, in the end a real win will emerge. It might not come immediately or the way you expect it, but it will come. We all have a part to play, however small we believe our contribution to be. One young English football player played his part in the summer of 2020.

Values-led activism

During the summer of 2020 the global COVID-19 pandemic was severely impacting families from low socioeconomic backgrounds across the UK. Marcus Rashford, the Manchester United and England centre forward footballer started a campaign to end food poverty. Marcus successfully lobbied the British government, forcing it to overturn a previous decision withholding funding for free school lunches for the children most in need over the summer school holidays. Due to his extraordinary campaigning efforts Marcus provided food for some of the nation's poorest families. Twenty-three-year-old Marcus achieved this through the power of his reach and in part due to his 9 million Instagram and 4 million Twitter followers. This is an historic first in the UK. No other British athlete had previously been able to use their influence to force the government to do a U-turn on social policy.

This all serves to show how change can be accelerated by 'Movements and Moments' coming together and through one person's individual will.

Individual free will and self-reliance underpins self-determination. The essence of self-determination is using your individual freedoms to determine your choices and success without outside influences. This philosophy is often associated with Black nationalism through the teachings of Marcus Garvey, Kwame Ture (formerly known as Stokely Carmichael) and Malcolm X. Self-determination says that we don't need others to define what it means for us to be liberated. There's no denying that none of us has complete self-determination or control over every aspect of our lives, with limits imposed by everything from the government deciding how much tax we have to pay to family responsibilities. But you do have some degree of power to increase what you *can* control, with many of us completely underestimating how much power we actually hold.

Historically, Black people have made collective choices to organize in Black-only spaces while also working alongside other organizations representing different ethnic and racial groups. This is still very much in affect today. Some Black communities, not served by the mainstream in their industry, choose to self-organize for their own political, social and moral purposes – for example starting businesses, charities and grassroots projects specifically aimed at catering to the needs of Black communities. Today in sport and media some of the organizations that encapsulate this self-determining approach include the Nutmegs football community for non-binary Black and

Brown women, the Football Black List, the Black Swimming Association, Blakademik TV, Goals4Girls and *SEASON* zine. Self-determination is linked to your choices. The leaders of these organizations decided to not be dictated to by the boundaries of marginalization. They each made a conscious choice to use their own personal agency to redress the imbalance on their terms. At any given moment you have the power to make a choice. Choosing to conform or not to societal norms is a choice and your choices are based on your fundamental core values.

The reason why Marcus Rashford was so passionate about food hunger is because he had experienced it himself: from a working-class background, he understands what it means to feel hunger. He can speak authentically from the pain and trauma of his experiences; people from similar backgrounds believe him because he has walked in their shoes. This is especially relevant when we know that 41 per cent of children live in a moderately or severely food-insecure UK household. Marcus uses his platform to always pay tribute to his mother's sacrifice which enabled him to become the footballer he is today. Rashford believes in compassion and that, as he wrote in a 'letter to his 10-year-old self' in the British newspaper *The Guardian*, 'kindness is power'. When your values and beliefs are aligned to your own forms of activism or campaigning, you are motivated and inspired to create change from a deeper place of authentic connection to the cause, because your identity is so firmly rooted in that issue or inequality. This can be achieved only when you know the values you stand for; forensically analysing what these values mean for you enables you to become strategic in how you overcome barriers and promote the issues that are important to you through your activism efforts.

Do we really know what we are prepared to stand for and why? Recognizing your own values as part of your campaigning efforts helps to build a sense of innate confidence and fearlessness, and it's this that provides the bedrock for success. Not all activism is about big protests, grand symbolic gestures, placards or massive publicity campaigns. Activism can be, and often is, the behind-the-scenes politicking and the small consistent daily actions of resistance and challenge that you are comfortable taking on in your professional and personal settings.

Tools of resistance

Aligning your values and personality type with your own form of activism in your professional and personal lives maximizes its impact.

Activism roles

Finding your social change role(s) is part of finding your authentic 'activism' voice. This can be dependent on characteristics and personality traits. Those of us who are more extrovert in nature may well find it easier to publicly call out social injustices than people with more introverted personality traits. Those people may be more comfortable quietly, yet just as powerfully, mobilizing communities and organizing collective responses to social injustice. Or there's the accidental activist, the person who previously was not that politicized but who, when injustice directly negatively impacts their life, are fired up to be part of the movement for change. In October 2020, as part of the FARE Network Football People Action weeks, I interviewed Michael Sam, the first publicly openly gay player in the American National Football League. He talked about how he had not been involved or known much about LGBTQ+ rights before he came out as gay. It was only after having come out publicly and faced extreme homophobia that Michael became more aware of the barriers facing his community and became an advocate and campaigner for LGTBQ + rights. I believe that sports activism and the different kinds of roles you choose to play can provide you with a starting point of how to apply this to challenging oppression in your everyday life as a part of a social change ecosystem.

Below I've drawn on the behaviours and attitudes of some of my favourite athletes who I think exemplify some of the main 'activist styles'. There are, of course, many other athlete activists who have made a mammoth contribution to social causes, and you, too, will have your own favourite role models you look to inside or outside the sporting world. The lesson I learned from listening to a podcast featuring one of Britain's most loved athletes, 400m hurdler Kriss Akabusi, is the power of not just looking up to role models but 'looking into' them as well. We can't always get close to our role models in the way Kriss Akabusi did when he trained with the legendary 400m hurdler Edwin Moses, but we can look into their behaviours and even channel ourselves through them, as we draw inspiration from their actions to create and make change. I cite these role models to inspire you to follow their lead and find ways to implement your own activism style aligned to your personality type.

POSITIVE DISRUPTOR

- Can you take uncomfortable actions to challenge the status quo?
- How can you embrace your role as a Serena Williams–style positive disruptor?
- Can you interpret this into your own activism efforts by being strategic in your behaviour, especially at key moments?
- Consider learning from others in your family or workplace who have challenged some form of oppression – what can you discard/keep in their approaches and adapt to your activism personality style?
- How can your behaviour stand for your values/the cause while not verbally saying anything (e.g. symbolic gestures, clothing, actions, performances)?
- Which organizations do you or your organization donate to, and how do you share and promote this information to give support and add strength to those campaigning for social justice?
- How can you create sustainability and legacy through your activism?
- Are you using mentoring strategies to inform, uplift and teach others?

POSITIVE DISRUPTORS IN SPORT

Serena Williams, Coco Gauff and Naomi Osaka, individually knowing the power in their reach, connecting with the Black Lives Matter movement and using their platforms inside and outside of sport to campaign for justice: Osaka by wearing five masks for five Black people in the USA murdered at hands of the police force; Williams by investing in social justice campaigns.

Tennis sports activism built on this interdependence of legacy and powerful visible role modelling: Althea Gibson, Serena Williams, Naomi Osaka and Coco Gauff.

EMPATHETIC STORYTELLER

- Are you a storyteller, crafting and sharing the truths on behalf of oppressed groups?
- Do you stand with and for other oppressed groups to highlight the interdependence of championing equity for all?
- When was the last time that you spoke up for another marginalized group (not your own) in a meeting?
- Can you work/team up with peers/family members to collectively convey a message of solidarity or challenge to highlight inequities for people from marginalized groups?
- Do you have diversity in your friendship or professional peer groups? If not, what can you do to diversify these groups?
- In your professional setting, how does your organization use key moments to highlight inequalities or value difference? For example, as a minimum does your organization celebrate LGBTQ+ month or Black History Month? Does your organization leadership intentionally connect with particular ethnic and cultural groups, acknowledging global events that maybe disproportionately impact their communities?

EMPATHETIC STORYTELLERS IN SPORT

Crystal Dunn, Megan Rapinoe, WNBA – Renee Montgomery, Maya Moore. US football and basketball teams are examples of teams collectively working together to fight intersectional oppression and campaign for social justice including greater parity for women's sport – demonstrating the power of collective action, agency and activism.

Simone Biles uses her voice to speak out against sexual assault in gymnastics, promoting and enacting out positive athlete mental health and welfare.

VISIONARY

- Do you have what it takes to go it alone, aiming for the boldest goals and possibilities?
- Can you take on huge corporations or leadership teams? This comes at a risk, though finding allies or external organizations with the same agenda as you can increase your influence and impact.
- Can you develop new collaborations and partnership with external organizations committed to the same principles?
- If you have a tricky meeting to navigate, could you engage your allies, enlisting their support to raise the issues on your behalf.
- If you are a leader in an organization, do you work in solidarity with marginalized communities, be that by seeking out job applicants from outside the bubble of white privilege to questioning the chairperson on the lack of diverse board representation?

VISIONARIES IN SPORT

Muhammad Ali, Marcus Rashford, Caster Semenya and Eniola Aluko have affected and changed international and national government social policy, setting a precedent for others to follow and creating a visible pathway. Athletes working with established advocacy organizations to campaign for mutual causes. Role modelling – challenging the status quo in the leadership of the country. Collaborating externally with charities/organizations using their assets to create a bigger impact.

WEAVER

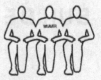

- Can you see lines of connectivity between people, organizations and movements?
- Do you use your institutional knowledge of practice, policies and behaviours in comparison to external good practice to highlight the inequitable outcomes in place for marginalized groups?
- Can you make a commitment to yourself to get comfortable calling out and challenging racism and other forms of oppression when you hear it from friends and family?
- Do you hold yourself accountable by setting personal targets to challenge oppression when you see it?
- Are you aware of the consequences of calling out oppression, especially if you're from a marginalized group (as highlighted in Chapter 1)? To support yourself increase your resilience tools of self-care.

WEAVER ACTIVISTS IN SPORT

Raheem Sterling – the Manchester City footballer called out the bigotry of the British media press and how its portrayal of Black players fuels racism on the terraces. The front-page images he used perfectly demonstrated the stereotypes and tropes associated with Black men.

In 2016 NFL American football player, Colin Kaepernick knelt during the US National Anthem, as a respectful way of calling on his country to protect and uphold the rights of all its people (#TakeAKnee). Kaepernick's protests relate to the killings of African Americans and minorities at the hands of an increasingly militarized police force in the United States. He has not played in the NFL since effectively being subject to constructive dismissal.

BUILDER

- Can you develop, organize and implement ideas, practices, people and resources in service of a collective vision?
- Is your activism skillset best suited to setting up or becoming part of an organization that challenges stereotypes and creates opportunities for the oppressed group?
- Have you considered whether your activism efforts are better best placed external to your workplace rather than inside it?
- Could you use your commitment, influence and personal agency to create your own solution to what you see as the problem?
- Could you set up a network/book club/charity/social enterprise to champion social justice issues?
- Have you considered writing articles to highlight injustice and inequality and getting them published in national and local media, or aligning your specific skillset to your social justice passion (e.g., as an accountant you could become the treasurer of your local disability rights group)?

BUILDER ACTIVISTS IN SPORT

Alice Dearing, Great Britain's first Black Olympic swimmer at the 2020 Tokyo Olympic Games, bulldozing archaic stereotypes that Black people can't swim. Alice used her agency to co-found the Black Swimming Association. In doing this, Alice became an activist campaigner, taking her passion and identity and creating a sustainable infrastructure to support others like her. Alice epitomizes self-determination.

Once you've decided on your activism style and type, you can plan your action. Using the following framework you can strategically plan your big and small activism efforts. Find your alignment, flow and enjoy the ride.

WHAT	TYPE	HOW
Decide on what you want to challenge and change and be clear about your rationale. Only then commit to your activism/action.	Decide on the kind of activist action – identify how it aligns with your style and personality and choose your social change/activism style/role.	Identify how, when and to whom – understand individual versus collective activism power and the importance of timing.
SIZE	**STRATEGY**	**RESOURCES**
Is it a big action/event or a series of ongoing actions?	What is your strategy for implementation and delivery? (short-term and longer-term vision/goals)	What resources do you need and who do you need to collaborate with? (target your champions)
IMPACT	**PREVENTATIVE**	**FUTURE**
What are the potential negative and positive outcomes locally and globally and how might these affect you?	What are the resilience traps you could fall into? What self- care tools will you adopt as part of your act(s) of resistance?	How will you increase, maintain and sustain momentum? (knowing the end game/bigger picture)

The impact of activism

When former professional footballer Eniola Aluko took on the UK Football Association (FA) at the Department for Digital, Culture, Media & Sport (DCMS) enquiry into racial discrimination and bullying (2017), many people supported her in this quest, including me. Eniola and fellow footballers Lianne Sanderson and Drew Spence experienced racism in the form of racist comments and stereotyping under the England Manager of the time, Mark Sampson. The same year I was awarded with an eminent Football Black List award for services to the community, and I dedicated this to Eniola. On receiving my award, my acceptance speech focused on her courage and her resilience in resolutely challenging the leaders of football and in so doing representing all Black women working in football and sport.

As a Black woman navigating the intersections of both structural inequalities of racism and sexism and in ultimately succeeding, she became a history maker and pioneer. The significance of Eniola's 'small axe' (one individual up against the might of the FA) actions serves to show women, and Black women in particular, that they are not invisible, that their voices count, that they can stand in their power and be counted and ultimately triumph. Eni showed us that the truth should be uncompromising. Her actions served to embolden and sustain Black women to own and use their power and agency. However, there were and continue to be real-life consequences for her. In her autobiography, *They Don't Teach This*, Eniola shares that when she decided to tell her story she knew she would be sacrificing her England career. Despite impressive form in 2018, playing for Juventus F.C. Women when it won the League and Cup double and finishing the season as the club's top scorer, Eniola never played for England again.

Black athletes who take on an activist role like Eniola by embracing their identity and taking public, political and antiracist positions can sadly expect punishment in some form or the other. This harsh retribution can be dealt out by the sport's governing body, brands, the media and social media, sponsors, teammates and fans. This can also apply to other forms of oppression, from sexism to ablism. Taking on a campaigning role can often result in an athlete being labelled as difficult, not being selected for national teams, sponsorship deals falling through and a loss of funding. Having said this, it does depend on the timing and particular context of the environment. For example, during the height of the Black Lives Matter movement in the summer of 2020 *The Daily Telegraph*, a conservative British broadsheet newspaper, dedicated a whole 16-page supplement on women's sport to the voices of Black women in sport and their negative experiences of racism and discrimination. I was nervous for some of these Black sportswomen using their voices to articulate their views on the Black Lives Matter movement and highlight the discrimination they have experienced. I couldn't help wondering whether, come the postponed Tokyo Olympic Games, they would somehow be penalized, or, worse, mysteriously dropped from a team for spurious reasons. One thing we know for sure is, as a friend once told me, racism is patient.

Jesse Owens, Muhammad Ali and Althea Gibson are testaments to this: when Black athletes choose to use their voices for greater racial equity, there is a direct negative impact on their lives and future livelihoods. This exclusion and rejection are much the same for anyone from a marginalized identity calling out injustice of some kind. When standing for an issue that the dominant culture within an organization or family context refuses to accept, you can experience exclusion in much the same ways athletes do. This might be by being excluded from strategic decisions at work that you might previously have been party to, or by being exiled from at least a part of your family. This can all have a detrimental and debilitating impact on your mental health. It's no surprise that UK rates for depression and mental health anxiety are higher for Black people than all other ethnic groups.

Sport symbolically shows us this, through the struggle and protest of athletes prepared to sacrifice themselves so they can become agents of change, hope and inspiration. As Nelson Mandela said way back in 2000 at the inaugural Laureus World Sports Awards: 'Sport has the power to change the world. It has the power to inspire. It has the power to unite people in a way that little else does. [...] Sport can create hope where once there was only despair.'

Tools of resistance

Athletes are driving governmental policy change and leading social movements far beyond the field of play.

The work of being an activist is the work of being an active and conscious citizen who cares deeply about humanity. It requires a strength of character to resist the internal dialogue that can at times trick your consciousness into almost believing things can never change: 'What's the point? Why not just accept it? The price I'll pay is just too massive.' This sentiment needs to be fought against with all your might. This chapter has shown you some of the individuals who have used their 'small axes' in big and transformational ways. Some of the biggest moments of social change in the UK, from the abolition of slavery to the achievement of women's suffrage, have all embryonically grown from individual activism. Signing up to be an activist in its broadest sense is, I believe, how you can play your part in changing your small part of the world. If athletes and activists can do this, then so can we as individuals and stars in our own lives, using our own influence, power and agency, because these are all facets of our professional and personal lives that we have control over. Whether you choose to adopt Caster Seymanya's fortitude, the Lawrences' courage and dedication, or Ali's strength and power is up to you and you alone. One thing we know for sure is that activism, movements, agitation, collective and shared responsibility all have a place in the pursuit for equality and justice.

Real wins

- Finding your voice can be a socially active and political act when used for more than just yourself.

- Activism is about the small and big moments of challenge while being fully aware of the personal and organizational sacrifices you may need to make.

- Identifying your activism style and signing up to be a social justice changemaker is an opportunity which is accessible to each and every one of us.

Epilogue: New realms

As we approach the finish line, I'm reminded why I started writing this book. I was a plus one! But not just any old plus one. I was a guest of my friend the sports journalist Anna Kessel, author of *Eat, Sweat, Play: How Sport Can Change Our Lives.* It was a gloriously rare hot day in south-west London, and under a cloudless blue sky we were sitting on Centre Court watching Serena Williams lose to Simona Halep in the final of the 2019 All England Lawn Tennis Championships. We are both die-hard Serena fans so it was excruciating torture to witness. Serena had obviously not received the memo that this was my first time watching her play on Centre Court because her performance was not matching the happy ending of my expectations. The spectators bubbled with nervous excitement, wonder and barely concealed disappointment that Serena was having a major off day. If I crooked and stretched my neck enough and peered through the crowds, I could see that there were just a handful of Black and Brown faces.

As I watched Serena (my heart slowly bleeding out) make unforced error after error, I played out the game, set and match of my own successes and failures in my mind's eye. I took a moment to revel in the fact that sport has taught me to not be defeated by one loss because ultimately it is your response and subsequent action that will determine your true success and wins in life. It was at that moment that I confided in Anna my aspirations to write a book, and it was her emphatic response of encouragement that sealed the deal. Serena's loss on court that day was my real win and the start of this journey.

Now we are coming to the end of that journey, I want you to be left with a deeper sense of your leadership power and agency to achieve your idea of success despite the barriers you might be facing. Endings can be sad, sometimes joyful and at other times it can be a case of 'Well, I'm glad *that*'s over.' If you're reading this then, I'm hopeful that you're in the first camp. Goodbyes are important, and this is why.

When I left my first job as a primary school teacher in a small inner-city London school the headteacher gave me a thank-you card which conveyed his heartfelt thanks for my contribution in challenging the school to think differently about race. His words were a complete surprise to me. From my very first day as the only Black teacher my values were challenged by the mere fact of being me. As a newly qualified teacher, I tentatively challenged the racial inequalities I saw while providing some of the solutions, but never felt I was having any real impact. Perhaps this is something you can relate to in your work because at times we can all can feel as if the contribution we make, day in day out, doesn't add up to anything of real substance or magnitude. The words in that card told me something different, that I *had* made a difference, that my efforts were felt, seen and valued. It was the perfect goodbye.

Throughout our real wins journey together, I've been challenging yet supportive, holding you to account yet compassionate and, above all, positive. This gift of mine comes wrapped in paper stamped with the words FOR YOUR URGENT ATTENTION. There's immediacy in my every word here: let's get on with this, let's take action in whatever way works for us. I urge you to honour your leadership journey by harnessing your talents and playing the starring role in the box-office hit that is your life. Your 'Tools of resistance' are your resilience fuel as you make the conscious choices to step up and step out. When patriarchy and oppression do their worst, the insider, outsider, outlier in me will, while being mindful of my own self-care, challenge the status quo because that's a part of who I am. Figuring out your part to play is just as important as the part you play. My advice is to live out your 'activist style' and rinse this for all it's worth, as that's when you know you've nailed your part. We all have a part to play – not only stepping up for ourselves in terms of professional and personal growth but in playing a social change role in fighting inequalities – the role is the 'part' you play.

I had to tap into my personal power in writing this book, with a clear execution plan just as I used to have for my races. However, as the words started to flow, I soon realized that I had to ditch my plan and serve up the stories that emerged in the most authentic way I knew how. So, I committed to whole-heartedly sharing more of my truths and to honour the shared experiences and lessons from the people I interviewed. This revealed the ways in which society is changing and therefore the ways in which how we lead is changing.

We have seen that effective leadership is grounded in authenticity, self-awareness and empathy for yourself and others. At its best, leadership is not about status or titles but realizing potential in yourself and those around you, while understanding your strengths and offering them up to be of service to your communities. We have uncovered what's involved in living a life beyond the limited vision of conventional social norms, and that by operating outside these margins is where we get to define our own real wins.

Not all of this applies equally, of course. There is an urgent need for leaders to stop being, as Professor Ibram X. Kendi puts it, 'racism deniers' and instead go about the untidy and unglamourous work of creating antiracist outcomes and protocols in workplaces. To be a conscious leader, to borrow the mighty words of Lola Young, Baroness Young of Hornsey OBE, you have to decide to be 'an agent for world benefit'. This applies both to your profession and to the business of your personal growth. We are (unfairly for some) all in it together, and so it becomes all our responsibilities to tackle racism and oppression. It is only then that organizational leaders, by creating inclusive cultures with a focus on conscious leadership, will enable everyone to play their 'leader-ful' part. In our transformation and success we are all interdependent.

Audre Lord, the American civil rights' activist, author and poet, reminds us that revolution is not, as she puts it, 'a one-time event'. Revolution can and should be present every day of our lives. It can be found in the smallest acts such as learning to respect the difference we perceive in others. We are, after all, bound by our common interest in survival and in order to survive we need to learn to differentiate between and choose to work with the groups or coalitions that most speak to our goals, even when those coalitions we may encounter bring a level of discomfort and don't fully resonate with our values. There will be parts of this book that you have unequivocally rejected and other parts where you've nodded in agreement recollecting a similar experience you may have had. My encouragement to you is to be intentional and strategic. You must implement your own strategic resistance plans in your life.

Your power is your responsibility. I say this with love and respect. To take power requires you to move your life in the direction of your boldest dreams. The very point of real wins is to help you get even better at getting what you want, to afford yourself the opportunity to grow and dare to be more ambitious in your demands for your personal and professional growth. Despite the access codes of privilege, you can take and find your power outside of what historic and societal boundaries dictate by redefining success *on your terms*. As with any change, this will absolutely involve a level of discomfort and anxiety, but if you choose to persevere, to release yourself from fear and the burden of the ultimate outcome, it's this willingness to stay the course that will intensify your firepower.

At different points in this book, I've used the word 'radical' to elicit a sense of revolution, of progressive thought, sweeping action and profound change. I want you to realize that a self-determining philosophy is open to every one of us with marginalized identities; because even when oppression and societal stereotypes try their best to limit your opportunities and potential, we can find individual and collective strength in community, in fellowship and a celebration of our full identities. Finding ways to connect with your community can be the most uplifting and empowering part of your identity. That sense of belonging that I got when I joined my athletics training group all those years ago was heightened because it was a *Black* training group. We all need our tribe where we feel seen, heard and understood.

The imperfect truth

One piece of feedback I received from a friend when I shared the news that I was writing a book was that he was confused about my message; 'It needs to be about one thing', he said, 'People can only understand one thing at a time, Michelle.' As he is an author himself, I had to give him his dues, but my response was immediate: 'It can't be because my life and the world are never about one thing and one thing alone.' We live in a complex world with big societal ills that need intricate, multifaceted solutions. That's where you, the reader, come in because complex problems need resolution in many different ways. Figuring out your real wins is a part of those solutions. This involves your own work of self-discovery, which I hope this book will have helped you with, developing your consciousness and creating awakenings which will drive you to be part of change. As Angela Davis says, 'I am no longer accepting the things I cannot change, I'm changing the things I cannot accept.' This is an ambition we would all do well to live into. For my white readers, being open to the challenge of racism, cognizant of the lived experiences of Black people, while acknowledging complicity, becomes the race to the finish line to *try* to change the things you cannot accept. I absolutely resist racism and oppression and *try* to use my leadership power, agency and influence to change the things I cannot accept. I don't always succeed, but there is a ferocity in my efforts. Taking this one step further by finding your space to resist, both inside and outside of organizations, becomes the space where you can practise your best leadership.

As a Black woman reconciling the tensions between the cycles of oppression is problematic. On the one hand, we all have agency; on the other hand, racism robs Black people of that agency which requires us to exercise our leadership in different ways. In many ways the examples from sport demonstrate this. I can't change the height of the netball post or the distance of the 400m race, and these are the hard facts. Black leaders have to become resilient in their fortitude in developing the mindset and self-determining approach to tackle what can sometimes feel and seem like an insurmountable terrain. Doreen Lawrence, in sharing her wisdom about Black mothers and their pain, speaks powerfully on this theme (and in a way with which I can strongly relate to): 'We achieve everything not because we are superhuman. We achieve the things we achieve because we are human. Our strength does not come from not having any weaknesses, our strength comes from overcoming them.'

What I know for sure is that truth wins every time. Truth matters – for yourself and for others. Organizational leaders must face the truth and reckon with the structural racism that exists in their professional environments. Once you know the experiences, the question becomes, what are leaders prepared to do about it? In November 2020 former US president Barrack Obama travelled to the UK as part of his book tour for his autobiography, *The Promised*

Land. Historian David Olusoga interviewed Obama for the BBC. A standout moment that struck a chord with me was when Obama articulated the complexities of holding the two or more paradoxical concepts or ideas in your head at the same time. He explains that sometimes your decisions as a leader will be imperfect but that doesn't mean a better decision can't be made in that moment. In other words, even though you can't make as many of the perhaps sweeping changes you want, you can always find a better way and bend yourself in the direction to a common creed even when the nature of the progress will create an inevitable backlash.

This makes me think about the conversations I have in which leaders or people more generally say they don't know what to do to tackle racial inequality. If we take Obama's teachings here and overlay them with a sense of urgency, then taking action, even if it's not perfect, becomes the work. The restoration of equity across all facets of oppression is paramount, and although this book has been dedicated to the Black experience of exclusion, this cannot come at the cost of other groups.

When you redress inequities for the most marginalized or vulnerable, all people in society benefit. Intersectional oppression is central to this. An interview with Paralympian and disability campaigner Anne Wafula Strike as part of ITV's Black History Month special programming highlighted this:

'When I was in Africa, the only thing that I had to fight was being a woman and having a disability. Then, I moved to the UK in the year 2000. I realized that I wasn't just a disabled woman, I was actually

disabled, female and Black. I have these intersection-
alities to deal with, so I know what it means to have
all these three things against you, I know what it
means to be at the bottom and not at the top, I know
what it means to be an afterthought. I know what it
means when doors are shut in your face because of
the colour of your skin, because you are female and
because you have a disability. I can't sit and wait for
somebody else to fight my battles. I have to go out
there and fight these battles myself.'

Anne shouldn't have to fight these battles alone, because
those battles belong to all of us. We should fight these battles with her and on her behalf. Anne represented Kenya in
wheelchair racing at the 2008 Paralympic Games and went
on to compete for Team GB at two World Championships.

As the masterful writer and activist James Baldwin
taught, when Black people are oppressed by White supremacy, that oppression also oppresses the humanity of white
people. Whether white people truly understand this or
prefer to remain in ignorance, it still stands that white
people who are unprepared to confront individual and
systemic racism while living in a largely white environment are unconsciously choosing to be an oppressor, robbing themselves of their full humanity in failing to fully
recognize the humanity of Black people. This becomes
about the oppression of one's mind. I've had to do it at
times in the writing of this book, literally decolonizing
my mind because part of my thinking has been framed
within whiteness and Western traditions. The liberation
of my thinking comes from using my power and agency
to make change, and this book has highlighted this in the

many ways I've chosen to use that currency. My question to you is: how will you use your power and agency to the benefit of yourself and your communities in challenging racial inequality and oppression in all its forms?

Start before you are ready

'This is not our first rodeo,' the acclaimed sports broadcaster and journalist Jessica Creighton reminded me when we had our interview about racism in sport and wider society. Jessica was and is correct. The statement landed differently with me this time. Maybe it's because right now in 2021 Britain, there seems to be more appetite to at least acknowledge that racism exists, or maybe it's because, now in my late forties, I fully understand the part I'm playing and have played over the decades.

In 2020, as Great Britain battled with the COVID-19 pandemic and the disproportionate impact it had on Black people and ethnic minority communities, in addition to the protests in response to George Floyd's racist murder, it seemed like the country was finally waking up to the dehumanizing, life-diminishing effects of racism on the lives of Black people. As organizations grappled with being called out for racism, urgent diversity action plans emerged. Before 2020 talking about racism in Britain was an epic non-event for those in power. There was always a lack of engagement; it was a bit like knocking on the front door knowing everyone's at home but not getting any answer. Since George Floyd's racist murder, acknowledging racism in wider public British discourse has become more socially acceptable. This is long overdue, and breaking open the engrained racism in British society and putting it on view has come at the cost of human life. If my tone here seems furious, sad and ungrateful all at the same time, you've read it correctly.

This is now a race against borrowed time. By 2050 one in five of the UK population will be from a Black or ethnic minority background. We are at moment in time when the wind is behind us and it is therefore incumbent upon us to maximize this opportunity if we are going to dismantle the chains of racial inequality. Otherwise, the wind may change direction and we will be blown far off course. This book has been about adding to the momentum and energy of our individual and collective leadership as it tackles racism and brings about real change in sport and wider society. My optimistic yet realistic ambition – I'm from South London, after all, so I do have my feet firmly planted on *terra firma* – is that we can all agree on the tenets of peace, justice and freedom, and that these are the right of every member of the Black community.

The baton of change that has passed from Tommie Smith and John Carlos, through Serena Williams and Colin Kaepernick, to Megan Rapinoe, Raheem Sterling, Naomi Osaka and Lewis Hamilton and beyond, demonstrates the power of sport activism. Sports activism can be a catalyst in creating transformative change for communities and in so doing present a vision for a more equitable landscape, one that benefits everyone. Throughout *Real Wins* I've challenged you to find your inner activist, much the same as these athlete activists have done, and to build upon and use their inspiration, energy and impetus to push the boundaries of your own personal and professional growth. Drawing on the inspiration of the activism of a Naomi Osaka or Raheem Stirling, decide on your changemaker role by finding your activist voice and aligning this to your passions, convictions and personality type to be the change you want to be and see in the world.

The challenges of twenty-first-century living are complex and therefore require you to be ambitious in your efforts, going beyond our own personal transformation to encompass the collective transformation and elevation of your communities. Whether your labours affect one or a hundred thousand people, everyone's efforts are valid and important in the pursuit of equality.

The answers within

My joy comes from inspiring, coaching, mentoring, strengthening and supporting people on their leadership journeys. I see this as playing my part in helping to create and manifest an ecosystem of warriors who are their own change agents in the world and who in turn will ignite fires in others to be part of the cycle for change. I'm passing that baton to you, so you can be the changemaker in your life and for your communities.

I had to adopt a winner's mentality in the writing of this book. To do this I had to understand that you are only as good as you think you are in any given moment. I had to draw on my inner self-belief system. Much like when, in the 2008 Beijing Olympic Games, Christine Ohuruogu, one of the UK's most decorated athletes, won the 400m in the last few strides of the most exciting and thrilling race of the games. I was screaming at the TV! It was magnificent – a moment that's forever etched in my consciousness as a classic example of sheer determination and grit. The victory was made even sweeter because Christine's training preparation had been plagued by injury throughout the year. It would have been easy for Christine to not even step onto the track at all, but she backed herself as a winner and brought home the gold medal. It's that which defines a winner's mentality. We can all back ourselves Ohuruogu style in the different aspects of our lives. As I hope you have learned from some of my life experiences I've written about in this book, so have I. In writing this book I have discovered new things about my own family history that have been uplifting and at times troubling. Revealing my truths is a vulnerable journey, yet without doubt I am grateful for the experience. My wish is that in narrating my stories I have enabled you to reconsider or maybe reshape your vision of success. And perhaps there has even been a shift in your worldview.

Through this writing there have been threads that I've deliberately left hanging because I'm very confident that I don't have all the answers. That said, I'm hopeful that I've increased awareness around issues of racial inequality in a way that has at least got some of you thinking, perhaps at first shaking your head in befuddlement, then receiving a sudden moment of clarity, and then finally taking inspired action – enabling you to offer your support, to say 'I see you. I hear you. I understand the unseen labour. I'm with you.' I have written this book from my lived experiences as a Black woman. I'm not a race theorist, academic or sociologist, though for the those of you who want to understand the ways in which capitalism, patriarchy and misogyny form the underbelly of racism there are many brilliant academics, authors and activists writing on this topic. I'd direct you to the writings of Afua Hirsch, Akala,

Audre Lorde, James Baldwin, Angela Davis, Laala Saad, Emma Dabiri and David Olusoga as your starting points, but there are many, many others.

I'm a former sprinter, and although it feels like we have just run a marathon together, my overall desire is that you've been touched, moved or inspired in some way and know that, in the end, we are all in this together. Resilience, weathering adversity and the real win lessons we learn along the way can become your very own blueprint for success. The world needs more of us who can be our best and give our best unblighted by the constructs of inequalities. You get to choose how you respond to the challenges of your lives, and in making these choices your real wins become real wins for you, your communities and the world.

The beauty of a book is that you get to pick it up again and again when you want to revisit the words of challenge, inspiration and advice it contains. My desire is that *Real Wins* will be that book which keeps on giving and which has an enduring impact. Right now, if we were together in person, I'd be saluting you with a knowing look that says 'I see you', and thanking you for choosing my book and investing your precious time in reading *Real Wins*. My departing head bop of respect would express that I'm rooting for you.

'Declaration of Independence' by Michelle Moore

A poem written in tribute to my paternal grandmother, Olga Moore, originally performed for The Declaration of Independence Performance Project for Barbara Asante, at the BALTIC Centre for Contemporary Arts, 23 February 2019.

I stand in the truths and on the shoulders of my personal histories and rich heritage.
In 1957 my nan took a voyage of discovery on a boat from Guyana to Great Britain with three young children –
One my dad.
My nan toiled and sacrificed for her family all in the name of love.
My nan survived the turmoil and legacy of a well-worn life of 93 years.
The harsh beauty of her courage, her resistance and ultimate empowerment has been passed down to me to embolden me in ways I don't truly realize.

*The memories of good times, of lessons learnt of
breaking bread and family traditions.
Coconut ice, fudge, fried fish, pepper sauce plentiful on
family celebrations – those joyful and special moments
that come from being held in her bosom, looked over,
cared over, loved.*

*Yet I feel the weight of injustice and oppression she
endured.
The fury, exhaustion and emotional labour of the Black
woman passed down through generations to one white
woman mother and two small Brown girls – my sister
and me.*

*It is my privilege and responsibility to honour this
weight of history and legacy of resilience.
To narrate my story using my agency and power to use
my independence to serve others in the way that has been
gifted to me.
Oppression and division are still the experiences of
Black women today.
Stepping up, activism, education and self-care are my
chosen weapons in this struggle.*

*The invisibility of the oppressed sticks in my throat
I can't back down when patriarchy and oppression do
their worse.
Insider, outsider, outlier challenging the status quo
that's me.
Fuelled by the fury of injustice and eloquent beauty
and liberation of rage aka Serena Williams style.*

Drawing on the strength of my heritage to sustain me
to take the risks, to go all in, despite the fear taking the
time to heal, to lament, to go again.
Self-love means speaking and standing in your truths
regardless of how uncomfortable it makes others feel.
Thank you, warrior Audre Lorde.

The pressure of conformity plays no part in my story
Unravelling and opposing the stereotype of being
less than to make others feel more than is just not my
gig. I refuse to be defined by the narrow constructs of
womanhood.
My boundaries are mine and mine alone to create and
redefine as I author the chapters of my own bestseller.

The freedom of independence affords me the luxury
of choice, of owning my success and revelling in winning
moments.
My joy comes from a job well done, when the
voices and faces of the young express their gratitude,
admiration, and innocence of thanks.
Replenishing my soul, igniting my passion, making
my heartbeat faster, my stride lighter and my chest high!
Supporting my sisters – sharing wisdom, creating abundance
and those divine moments of self-discovery.

Freedom, liberation, and independence on my terms
to live audaciously and vulnerably as Brené Brown says
'braving the wilderness'.
Aiming for that personal best, staying in my lane,
competing with myself, leaving everything on the track –
rinsing every drop out of this lifetime to honour my nan,
my nan, my nan ...

Endnotes

Introduction

Akala. 2018. *Natives: Race and Class in the Ruins of Empire*. London: Two Roads.

Chapter 1

Bandura, A. 1977. Self-efficacy: Toward a unifying theory of behavioral change. *Psychological Review* 84(2): 191–215. https://doi.org/10.1037/0033-295X.84.2.191

Brown, B. 2018. *Dare to Lead*. New York: Vermillion.

Carrington, B. 2010. *Race, Sport and Politics: The Sporting Black Diaspora*. Thousand Oaks, CA: SAGE.

Coughlan, S. 2021. Only 1% of UK university professors are black, *BBC News*, 19 January. Available at: www.bbc.co.uk/news/education-55723120

Covey, S. 2004. *The Seven Habits of Highly Effective People*. New York: Simon & Schuster.

Dweck, C. 2017. *Mindset: Changing the Way You Think to Fulfil Your Potential*, updated edn. London: Robinson.

Ingle, S. 2019. 'I've cried enough to last me a career': How adversity drove Johnson-Thompson to gold, *The Guardian*,

4 October. Available at: www.theguardian.com/sport/2019/oct/04/cried-enough-katarina-johnson-thompson-injuries-heartbreak-athletics-gold_

Itani, O. 2020. How to think like a champion: Michael Jordan's 8 'growth mindset' traits, *Mind Café*, 11 July. Available at: https://medium.com/mind-cafe/how-to-think-like-a-champion-michael-jordans-8-growth-mindset-traits-e9efca83469b

Goal. 2020. How many Black managers have coached Premier League clubs? *Goal.com*, 15 October. Available at: www.goal.com/en/news/how-many-black-managers-coached-premier-league-clubs/ho1anor6n5w41uf9dunlsxejg

Kelner, M. 2017. Katarina Johnson-Thompson's high jump flop hits heptathlon medal hopes. *The Guardian*, 5 August. Available at: www.theguardian.com/sport/2017/aug/05/katarina-johnson-thompson-world-championship-heptathlon-blow

PA Media. 2010. Raheem Sterling demands English football gives black managers a chance, *The Guardian*, 9 June. Available at: www.theguardian.com/football/2020/jun/09/raheem-sterling-english-football-black-managers-campbell-cole

Winfrey, O. 2017. Dr Michael Bernard Beckwith interview, *SuperSoul Conversations Podcast*, 25 October. Available at: www.youtube.com/watch?v=rorytNojYt8

Chapter 2

Begum, H. 2020. So the ethnicity pay gap is over? If only things were that simple, *The Guardian*, 15 October. Available at: www.theguardian.com/commentisfree/2020/oct/15/ethnicity-pay-gap-disparities-minority-workers-unemployed-precarious-work

Carrington, B. 2010. *Race, Sport and Politics: The Sporting Black Diaspora*. Thousand Oaks, CA: SAGE.

Crenshaw, K. 2019. Why intersectionality can't wait. Available at: www.gwi-boell.de/en/2019/05/20/why-intersectionality-cant-wait

Cooper, B. 2018. *Eloquent Rage: A Black Feminist Discovers Her Superpower*. New York: St. Martin's Press.

Greer, B. 2020 As the most powerful woman in US history, Kamala Harris will help black women like me look in the mirror, *The Daily Telegraph*, 9 November. Available at: www.telegraph.co.uk/women/politics/powerful-woman-us-history-kamala-harris-will-help-black-women/

Henry, L., and Ryder, M. 2021, *Access All Areas: The Diversity Manifesto for TV and Beyond*, London: Faber & Faber.

Home Office. 2019. Police workforce ethnicity facts and figures. Available at: www.ethnicity-facts-figures.service.gov.uk/workforce-and-business/workforce-diversity/police-workforce/latest

Home Office. 2020. School teacher workforce ethnicity facts and figures. Available at: https://www.ethnicity-facts-figures.service.gov.uk/workforce-and-business/workforce-diversity/school-teacher-workforce/latest#by20-ethnicity-and-role

Kwakye, J. 2020. As a black woman, you have to leave part of yourself back in the changing room — but attitudes are changing, *The Telegraph*, 25 June. Available at: https://www.telegraph.co.uk/athletics/2020/06/25/black-woman-have-leave-part-back-changing-room-attitudes-changing/

Makortoff, K. 2020. UK black professional representation 'has barely budged since 2014', *The Guardian*, 22 June. Available at: www.theguardian.com/business/2020/jun/22/uk-black-professional-representation-has-barely-budged-since-2014

Narween, G. 2020. Black business managers still under-represented, says study, *The Times*, 22 June. Available at: www.thetimes.co.uk/article/businesses-failing-to-promote-black-people-6w8jk2gg2

Office for National Statistics. 2019. Earnings and employment statistics. Available at: www.ons.gov.uk/employmentandlabourmarket/peopleinwork/earningsandworkinghours/articles/ethnicitypaygapsingreatbritain/2019

Office for National Statistics. 2020. Police powers and procedures: England and Wales. Available at: https://www.gov.uk/government/statistics/police-powers-and-procedures-england-and-wales-year-ending-31-march-2020

Race Disparity Audit. 2018. Summary findings from the ethnicity facts and figures website. Available at: https://assets.publishing.service.gov.uk/government/uploads/system/uploads/attachment_data/file/686071/Revised_RDA_report_March_2018.pdf October 2017 (revised March 2018)

Saad, L. 2020. *Me and White Supremacy: How to Recognise Your Privilege, Combat Racism and Change the World.* London: Quercus.

Steinmetz, K. 2018. Kimberlé Crenshaw speaks during the New York Women's Foundation's 'Celebrating Women' breakfast in New York City, *Time*, 10 May. Available at: https://time.com/5786710/kimberle-crenshaw-intersectionality/

Traister, R. 2018. Serena Williams and the game that can't be won (yet): What rage costs a women, *The Cut*, 9 September. Available at: www.thecut.com/2018/09/serena-williams-us-open-referee-sexism.html

Treloar, N., and Begum, H. 2021. *Facts Don't Lie: One Working Class: Race, Class and Inequalities Report*, The Runnymede Trust. Available at: www.runnymedetrust.org/uploads/publications/Facts%20Dont%20Lie%20(2021)-Begum%2C%20Treloar%20.pdf

TUC Equality Briefing. 2020. *BME Women and Work.* Available at: www.tuc.org.uk/research-analysis/reports/bme-women-and-work

Winfrey, O. 2013. Commencement address, *The Harvard Gazette*, 31 May. Available at: https://news.harvard.edu/gazette/story/2013/05/winfreys-commencement-address/

Chapter 3

Clance, P. R., and Imes, S. A. 1978. The impostor phenomenon in high achieving women: Dynamics and therapeutic intervention, *Psychotherapy: Theory, Research & Practice* 15(3): 241–7. Available at: http://mpowir.org/wp-content/uploads/2010/02/Download-IP-in-High-Achieving-Women.pdf

Hunt, V., and Prince, S. 2015. Why diversity matters, *mckinsey. com*. Available at: www.mckinsey.com/business-functions/ organization/our-insights/why-diversity-matters

Kendi, X. I. 2019. *How to be in Antiracist.* London: Penguin Random House.

Steel, C. 2011. *Whistling Vivaldi: How Stereotypes Affect Us and What We Can Do.* New York: W. W. Norton & Company.

Tulshyan, R., and Burey, J, 2021. Stop telling women they have imposter syndrome, *Harvard Business Review*, 11 February. Available at: https://hbr.org/2021/02/ stop-telling-women-they-have-imposter-syndrome

Chapter 4

Akpan, P. 2021. Why research and conversation about menopause is letting down Black and Asian people, *Good Housekeeping*, 16 February. Available at: www.goodhousekeeping. com/uk/health/a35000306/menopause-research-healthcare-letting-down-black-and-asian-people/

Brown, L. 2018. One of the greatest speeches ever, *MotivationHub*. Available at: www.youtube.com/watch?v=NQ4en7o8B-g

Fullerton, D. J., Zhang, L. M., and Kleitman, S. 2021. An integrative process model of resilience in an academic context: Resilience resources, coping strategies, and positive adaptation, *PLOS ONE*, 2 February. Available at: https://doi.org/10.1371/journal.pone.0246000

Hone, L. 2019. The three secrets of resilient people, *TEDx Talks*. Available at: www.youtube.com/watch?v=NWH8N-BvhAw

Packnett, B. 2018. Living at the intersection, The *New York Times* Talk. Available at: www.youtube.com/watch?v=HoDmEH47Xos&t=4s

Parke, P. 2020. 'The Meghan Markle effect', in Y. Adegoke and E. Uviebinené (eds), *Loud Black Girls: 20 Black Women Writers Ask: What's Next?* London: Fourth Estate.

Randone, A. 2020. Black, menopausal, and opinionated: How podcast host Karen Arthur found her voice, *Vogue*, December issue. Available at: www.vogue.co.uk/beauty/article/karen-arthur-interview

Thomas-Smith, A., and Young, G. 2020. Podcast transcript: Gary Young on the global Black Liberation uprisings, New Economics Foundation, 24 June. Available at: https://neweconomics.org/2020/06/weekly-economics-podcast-transcript-gary-younge-on-the-global-black-liberation-uprisings

Chapter 5

BBC Sport. 2020. Raheem Sterling speaks out on racism following the death of George Floyd, 8 June. Available at: www.bbc.co.uk/sport/football/52959292

BlackPast. 2012 [1982] Audre Lorde learning from the 60s. www.blackpast.org/african-american-history/1982-audre-lorde-learning-60s/

De Pree, M. 2004. *Leadership Is an Art*. New York: Currency Doubleday.

Ingle, S. 2020. Britain's sporting 'apartheid' must end, says Sport England's Chris Grant, *The Guardian*, 7 June. Available at: www.theguardian.com/sport/2020/jun/07/britains-sporting-apartheid-must-end-says-sport-englands-chris-grant

Johnson-Thompson, K. 2020. 'I've been a Black woman longer than I've been an athlete': On her personal battle against racism, *Vogue UK*, 30 August. Available at: www.vogue.co.uk/arts-and-lifestyle/article/katarina-johnson-thompson-racism

McGregor-Smith, R. 2018. *Race in the Workplace: The McGregor-Smith Review*. Available at: https://assets.publishing.service.gov.uk/government/uploads/system/uploads/attachment_data/file/594336/race-in-workplace-mcgregor-smith-review.pdf

Mos-Shogbamimu, S. 2020. Interview, *@CNN News*, 4 February. Available at: https://twitter.com/sholamos1/status/1224780414931427329?lang=en

Northouse, P. 2012. *Leadership: Theory and Practice*. Thousand Oaks, CA: SAGE Publications.

Seligman, N. 2019. *Conscious Leadership*. London: Quarto.

Sport England. 2020. Sport for all. Available at: www.sportengland.org/news/sport-for-all

Telegraph Sport. 2020. Special investigation: Just five black women among 415 leading sports board members, Telegraph Sport. Available at: www.telegraph.co.uk/womens-sport/2020/06/25/special-investigation-just-five-black-women-among-415-leading/

Thomas, F. 2019. Baroness Young criticises lack of BAME representation on Women's Super League Board, *The Daily Telegraph*, 25 July. Available at: https://www.telegraph.co.uk/womens-sport/2020/06/25/special-investigation-just-five-black-women-among-415-leading/

Women of the World Festival. 2017, Angela Davis in conversation, 11 March 2017. Available at: www.youtube.com/watch?v=lBgdzK3jfEg

Chapter 6

Asmelash, L., and Muaddi, N. 2019. Serena Williams says the day she stops fighting for equality 'will be the day I'm in my grave', *cnn.com*, 13 July. Available at: https://edition.cnn.com/2019/07/13/us/serena-williams-wimbledon-equality-trnd/index.html

BlackPast. 2012 [1982] Audre Lorde learning from the 60s. www.blackpast.org/african-american-history/1982-audre-lorde-learning-60s/

Bune, R., and Field, P. 2010. Mangrove Nine: The court challenge against police racism in Notting Hill, *The Guardian*, 29 November. Available at: www.theguardian.com/law/2010/nov/29/mangrove-nine-40th-anniversary

Cochrane, L. 2020. Burberry partners with Marcus Rashford to fund youth centres. Footballer publishes letter to his 10-year-old self to encourage people 'to dream', *The Guardian*, 2 November. Available at: www.theguardian.com/football/2020/nov/02/burberry-partners-with-marcus-rashford-to-fund-youth-centres

Gregory, S. 2017. Serena Williams finishes the fight for historic win at Australian Open, *Fortune*, 28 January. Available at: https://fortune.com/2017/01/28/serena-williams-australian-open/

Iyer, D. 2020. Mapping our roles in a social change ecosystem, Building Movement Project. https://buildingmovement.org/wp-content/uploads/2020/06/Final-Mapping-Ecosystem-Guide-CC-BY-NC-SA-4.0-Handles.pdf

James, M., and McKinley, C. 2017. Black-only meetings about self-determination, *The Philadelphia Inquirer*, 18 April. Available at: www.inquirer.com/philly/opinion/commentary/20170418_Commentary__Black-only_meetings_about_self-determination.html

Laureus. 2020. Nelson Mandela's sport has the power to change the world, Inaugural speech Laureus World Sports Awards. Available at: https://www.laureus.com/news/celebrating-the-legacy-of-a-hero-on-mandela-day

Lewis, J. 2014. Commencement Keynote Address, Emory University, 12 May. Available at: https://www.youtube.com/watch?v=EvD6Zfvih3g

Lorde, A. G. 1984. *Sister Outsider: Essays and Speeches.* Trumansburg, NY: Crossing Press.

Noah, T. 2020. George Floyd, Minneapolis protests, Ahmaud Arbery & Amy Cooper, The Daily Social Distancing Show, 29 May. Available at: www.youtube.com/watch?v=v4amCfVbA_c

Pereira, A. L., Handa, S., and Holmqvist, G. 2017. *Prevalence and Correlates of Food Insecurity among Children across the Globe.* UNICEF Office of Research, Innocenti Working Paper. Available at: www.unicef-irc.org/publications/pdf/IWP_2017_09.pdf

Zirin, D. 2013. *Game Over,* New York: The New Press.

Chapter 7

Baldwin, J. The Baldwin–Buckley Debate, University of Cambridge. 1965. Available at: www.youtube.com/watch?v=NUBh9GqFU3A

Davis, A. Y. 2016. *Freedom is a Constant Struggle: Ferguson, Palestine, and the Foundations of a Movement.* Chicago: Haymarket Books.

Henry, L., and Ryder, M. 2021. *Black British Lives Matter.* London: Faber & Faber.

ITV News. 2020. Black voices in conversation: Paralympian Anne-Wafula Strike on the intersection of race, gender and disability, ITV News, 30 October. Available at: https://www.itv.com/news/2020-10-30/black-voices-in-conversation-paralympian-anne-wafula-strike-on-the-intersection-of-race-gender-and-disability

Kendi, X. I. 2019, *How to be in Antiracist.* London: Penguin Random House.

Acknowledgements

One of the most unexpected parts about writing this book was the immense support I received from so many people known and unknown to me. It was touching and helped this book adventure feel less daunting because at times it's been an intense process. There's always a team behind any performance and the journey to writing this book has only been possible because of the quality and extraordinary relationships I am blessed to have in my life. I am truly grateful to the sharp minds and thoughtfulness of my professional and personal networks and the different tribes I belong to.

A huge thanks to the smart and brilliant people whom I have interviewed, many of whom are included in this book. Thank you for sharing your truths, wisdom, honesty and opening doors for me: Lola Young, Ama Agbeze, Chris Grant, Clarence Callendar, David Grevemberg, Denise Lewis, Donna Fraser, Donovan Reid, Ebony Rainford-Brent, Jeanette Kwakye, Colin Salmon, Eniola Aluko, Jessica Creighton, Kate Richardson-Walsh, Kevin Hylton, Tommie Smith, Laura Georges, Nova Reid, Benny Bonsu, Marcia Wilson, Pops Mensah-Bonsu, Ben Carrington, Kojo Mensah-Bonsu, Samantha Johnson, Bilqis Abdul

Qaadir, Shireen Ahemd, Jordan Jarrett-Bryan, Sanchez Bailey, Piara Powar, Zem Clarke, Jules Boykoff, Tanni Grey-Thompson, Tunji Akintokun, John Amaechi, Nikesh Shukla and Matthew Ryder. To those who helped me to start this writing journey, who have read my work and provided me with excellent insights, wise counsel and constructive criticism, thank you: Anna Kessel, Marcus Ryder and Hayley Bennett. Thanks to the superb writer and my friend Derek Bardowell not only for your guidance but for dropping everything and calling me to urge me to respond to my agent's email which I had sat on for three weeks. Many of my stories in this book span different parts of my life and so there are too many people to thank. So, this is a collective shoutout to all those people who have been a part of my journey and have helped me to unleash 'moore' of myself in these pages.

Special recognition to my agent, Rebecca Winfield, and the team at David Luxton Associates for believing in me from the very start. To the team at Nicholas Brealey, Hachette UK and my editor, Holly Bennion, for your patience and guidance with our lengthy conversations. To my sisterfriends who are the best cheerleaders of compassion and encouragement: heartfelt gratitude to Lesley McKenley, Tracy Reid and Tracey Sage. To the voices of the mentors in my head who inspire me: Maya Angelou, Oprah Winfrey, Brené Brown, Audre Lorde, Toni Morrison, Michelle Obama, James Baldwin, Serena Williams, Simone Biles, Muhammad Ali, John Carlos, Tommie Smith and Yvonne Lawrence. To my readers without whom none of this works – thank you for choosing me and my book. I'm grateful to be part of your journey.

Much respect, love and thanks to my family. For my mum, Ann: your sacrifice, patience and boundless love sustain me. To my dad, Peter, for making me feel like I can conquer Mount Everest. To my twin and favourite person, Françoise, for never doubting me, for lifting me up in your unwavering style and for always being in my corner. To my brother Jean Pierre for your wit and curiosity, and to my younger siblings, Christian and Kirsty: I appreciate your faith in me. Above all, I'm grateful to lead a life that enables me to honour the legacy of my grandparents, Olga and Vidal Moore and Margaret and Charlie Mace, to whom my thanks are endless.

About the author

© Andy Commons

Michelle Moore tirelessly champions a brand of conscious leadership for a new age of sport and business. She is a sought-after leadership coach, educator and international speaker with over two decades of experience leading national and international programmes at the intersections of sports and social change. Based on her extensive experience working in senior executive leadership and management roles across education, government and sport, her award-winning consulting and coaching work has transformed the lives of professionals, young people, athletes and the culture of many organisations. Michelle's coaching programmes focus on personal and collective transformation supporting individuals and organisations to achieve greater growth and performance. Her work has empowered hundreds of professionals and led her to become known for her authentic style as a well-known coach and connector.

Winner of the PRECIOUS Award for Outstanding Woman in Sport, a Football Black List award and a national Change Maker award, Michelle is a globally recognized executive on leadership, race equity and sport for development. She works with corporate, government, charities, international and national sport federations and businesses at a leadership level to create solutions steeped in strategic insight and cultural context. Michelle is a Guardian Masterclass leadership tutor.

Michelle enjoys an international public-speaking career delivering keynotes on leadership, equity, resilience and success. As a respected voice for equality in sport she has chaired high-profile sports panels and curated, convened, and moderated numerous events, roundtables and conferences for government, anti-discriminatory initiatives and advocacy organisations. These include chairing events at the United Nations and presenting to the House of Lords.

Michelle regularly appears in the media including BBC Radio 4, TRT World and Channel 4 and has been featured in *The Guardian, The Daily Telegraph, The Times* and *The Independent*. She also holds a number of non-executive roles in sport and is a Senior Honorary Associate lecturer at the University of Worcester. She is a regular contributor on BBC Radio London.

Michelle grew up with her twin sister in South London in the South of England. She loves watching live sport and travelling and preferably doing both at the same time. She enjoys her godchildren and is described as the coolest auntie. Michelle lives in London.

Would you like your people to read this book?

If you would like to discuss how you could bring these ideas to your team, we would love to hear from you. Our titles are available at competitive discounts when purchased in bulk across both physical and digital formats. We can offer bespoke editions featuring corporate logos, customized covers, or letters from company directors in the front matter can also be created in line with your special requirements.

We work closely with leading experts and organizations to bring forward-thinking ideas to a global audience. Our books are designed to help you be more successful in work and life.

For further information, or to request a catalogue, please contact:
business@johnmurrays.co.uk

Nicholas Brealey Publishing is an imprint of
John Murray Press.